Mornings
with Mary

Mornings
with Mary

SELECTED AND EDITED BY THE
EDITORS OF SERVANT PUBLICATIONS

CHARIS

SERVANT PUBLICATIONS
ANN ARBOR, MICHIGAN

© 1997 by Servant Publications

Charis Books is an imprint of Servant Publications especially designed to serve Roman Catholics.

Acknowledgments are located at the end of the book.

Published by Servant Publications
P.O. Box 8617
Ann Arbor, Michigan 48107

Cover design: Left Coast Design, Portland, OR
Cover photograph: Marco Basaiti/Superstock/Fine Arts. Used by permission
Interior photographs: Planet Art, Raphael and Botticelli collections

97 98 99 00 10   9 8 7 6 5 4 3 2 1

Printed in Mexico
ISBN 0-89283-995-3

LIBRARY OF CONGRESS CATALOGING-IN-PUBLICATION DATA

Mornings with Mary / selected and edited by the editors of Servant Publications.
     p.   cm.
   ISBN 0-89283-995-3
   1. Mary, Blessed Virgin, Saint—Meditations.   2. Mary, Blessed Virgin, Saint—
   Prayer books and devotions—English.   3. Mary, Blessed Virgin, Saint—Literary
   collections.   4. Mary, Blessed Virgin, Saint—Biography.   5. Mary, Blessed
   Virgin, Saint—Poetry. I. Title
   BT608.5.M68   1997
   232.91—dc21   97-13523
                                                              CIP

Introduction

P ainters, poets, ponderers, preachers. For nearly two thousand years they've been telling the story of the God who chose to become One of us—born as a fleshy child. Jesus remains the central character, and yet the story doesn't work apart from the daughter of Eve, Mary, who was ready and willing to accept the maternal mission as sketched out (in the barest of details) by a grand messenger, the archangel Gabriel.

After the nativity narratives, the Scriptures themselves give few glimpses into Mary's life. But at the end of two vignettes, Luke's gospel says she pondered the events, mulling the mysteries she didn't fully understand.

There's much about the story we still don't understand. On top of the basic scriptural account, Catholic and Orthodox tradition has laid its stones. Preachers have found their points. Poets have set their metaphors. Visionaries have stood and stretched to catch a glimmer of glory. In this collection you'll find a sampling of such classic and contemporary reflections on Mary. As the title suggests, you might read a selection each morning. Or you might browse—skimming any that don't strike you and marking others as favorites.

Like Mary, ponder the mysteries. And ask the Holy Spirit to draw you near to the heart of God.

Evelyn Bence

I

Contemplate the Simplicity

We have heard, endlessly and wearisomely, all the countless reasons why Mary "doesn't work" as a metaphor for our times and for our generation. We have heard the whimpers and the cries of rage, the anger and disillusionment; we have heard that Mary is too passive, too much of a people-pleaser; too weak, too virginal, too pure, too easily shaped, too obedient, too good to be true. All these complaints seem thin, and beside the point, when we contemplate the poetic simplicity of her girlish form, bending with tenderness over the child in the hay; when we experience the revolutionary power of her appearance among the poor and the oppressed; when we take into account her constant willingness to appear to simple folk in unlikely places, leaving behind her the waters of healing springs and roses that last on shawls for centuries; and when we hear her voice speaking (we don't know precisely how) in the inner reaches of our hearts, asking us to pray for the conversion of whole countries and continents, warning us to prepare for apocalyptic events; calling us, always, into the childlike simplicity we knew long ago when we lined up in rows to be shepherds and wise men, when we wove flowers and branches into May-crowns for pageants.

—*Emilie Griffin*

2

What Shall Bring Me Forward?

What shall bring me forward in the narrow way, as I live in the world, but the thought and patronage of Mary? What shall seal my senses, shall tranquilize my heart, when sights and sounds of danger are around me but Mary? What shall give me patience and endurance, when I am wearied out with the length of the conflict with evil, with the unceasing necessity of precautions, with the irksomeness of observing them, with the tediousness of their reception, with the strain upon my mind, with my forlorn and cheerless condition, but a loving communion with you!

You will comfort me in my discouragements, solace me in my fatigues, raise me after my falls, reward me for my successes. You will show me your Son, my God and my all. When my spirit within me is excited, or relaxed, or depressed, when it loses its balance, when it is restless and wayward, when it is sick of what it has, and hankers after what it has not, when my eye is solicited with evil and my mortal frame trembles under the shadow of the tempter, what will bring me to myself, to peace and health, but the cool breath of the Immaculate and the fragrance of the Rose of Sharon?

—*Cardinal John Henry Newman*

3

Christ's Mirror

Herself a rose, who bore the Rose,
　　She bore the Rose and felt its thorn,
　　All Loveliness new-born
Took on her bosom its repose,
　　And slept and woke there night and morn.

Lily herself, she bore the one
　　Fair Lily; sweeter, whiter, far
　　Than she or others are:
The Sun of Righteousness her Son,
　　She was His morning star.

She gracious, He essential Grace,
　　He was the Fountain, she the rill:
　　Her goodness to fulfil
And gladness, with proportioned pace
　　He led her steps thro' good and ill.

Christ's mirror she of grace and love,
　　Of beauty and of life and death:
　　By hope and love and faith
Transfigured to His Likeness "Dove,
　　Spouse, Sister, Mother," Jesus saith.

—*Christina Rossetti*

4

Without the Gospels

Paul's single recorded
allusion to Mary
is the one word
woman.
"Born of a woman," so he summed it up.

Which seems to show
that, valuable
as his epistles are,
we would be poor indeed
without the Gospels
and their humane portrayal
of the Christ Paul preached,
who took his first
uncertain steps
as Mary's little boy.

—*Thomas John Carlisle*

11

5

A Book Bearing the Word

You, O Mary,
have been made a book
in which our rule is written today.
In you today
is written the eternal Father's wisdom;
in you today
our human strength and freedom are revealed.
I say that our human dignity is revealed
because if I look at you, Mary,
I see that the Holy Spirit's hand
has written the Trinity in you
by forming within you
the incarnate Word, God's only-begotten Son.
He has written for us the Father's wisdom,
which this Word is;
he has written power for us,
because he was powerful enough
to accomplish this great mystery;
and he has written for us
his own—the Holy Spirit's—mercy,
for by divine grace and mercy alone
was such a great mystery
ordained and accomplished.

—*Catherine of Siena*

6

To the Mother of Graces

I greet you, Mother of Graces!… When I proclaim Christ, the Son of the living God, "God from God," "Light from Light," "of the same substance as the Father," at that moment I profess with the whole Church that He became man through the Holy Spirit and was born of the Virgin Mary. Your name, Mary, is indissolubly connected with His Name. Your call and your "yes" belong inseparably, therefore, from that moment onwards, to the mystery of the Incarnation.

With the whole Church I profess and proclaim that Jesus Christ in this mystery is the only mediator between God and man: for His incarnation brought to Adam's sons, who are subjected to the power of sin and death, redemption and justification. At the same time, I am deeply convinced [that] no one has been called to participate so deeply as you, the Mother of the Redeemer, in this immense and extraordinary mystery. And no one is better able than you alone, Mary, to let us penetrate this mystery more easily and clearly—we who announce it and form a part of it.

—*Pope John Paul II*

7

The Story Foretold and Fulfilled

St. Jerome ... says, "Death came by Eve; life by Mary."

Going back through the long vista of prophecies to the very cradle of the human race, when the voice of Jehovah awoke in the heart of fallen man a ray of hope, the Mother has her place with the Son in the Divine promise of salvation. No sooner had the sickly pall of sin tainted the fair face of the new creation, and our fallen parents had hidden in guilty fear among the trees of Paradise than God, in His mercy, promised a Redeemer.... [The] deceitful serpent had seduced the first woman, and through her brought ruin to the whole human race. Another woman was to crush the enemy's head, and to bring salvation to the fallen race.... "She shall crush thy head, and thou shalt lie in wait for her heel" (Gen. 3:14).

The centuries rolled by, and the prophets ... from time to time, made clearer and clearer the promise of the Redemption—the salvation which was to come through the second Eve....

St. John tells the sublime story of how the hidden mysteries of the Incarnation came to pass: "The Word was made Flesh, and dwelt among us, and we saw his glory ... " (John 1:14).

The story so long foretold in prophecy is fulfilled; and an angel-herald announces the gladsome news from the battlements of heaven.

—*J. A. M. Gillis, A.M.*

8

Adam Lay Ibounden

Adam lay ibounden,
bounden in a bond
four thousand winters
thought he not too long;
and all was for an apple,
an apple that he took,
as clerkes finden
written in their book.

Ne had the apple taken been,
the apple taken been,
ne had never our lady
been heaven's queen.
Blessed be the time
that apple taken was!
Therefore we may singen
Deo gracias.

—*Fifteenth-Century Carol*

9

Wonder at This . . .

Is it not startling to hear that the ineffable God, whom words cannot describe nor thought grasp, and who is in all things equal to the Father, was pleased to come to us through the womb of a virgin, to be made of a woman, and to take the forefathers David and Abraham? But why should I speak of David and Abraham? It is more astounding still that He took for ancestresses those women whom I have just named [including Tamar and Ruth]. But when you hear this, stir up your mind, and look not down upon the lowly elements. Wonder rather at this, that the very and beloved Son of the Eternal God was content to become the Son of David, that He might give you power to become a son of God; to have His own servant for His forefather, that He might make God His servants' Father.

—*Saint John Chrysostom*

10

The Joyful Mysteries

For centuries the chosen people of Israel waited for the coming of the Redeemer. Finally, "when the fullness of time had come, God sent his Son, born of a woman, born under the law, to ransom those under the law, so that we might receive adoption" (Gal 4:4-5, NAB).

The fulfillment of these prophecies and promises made to the chosen people began to be realized with the coming of Jesus, which is recorded in the nativity narratives of Matthew and Luke. This fulfillment is recalled in the joyful mysteries of the Rosary; the Annunciation, the visitation, the birth of Jesus, the presentation in the temple, the finding of the child Jesus in the temple....

These joyful mysteries call to mind the infinite goodness of the Lord in sending his Son to redeem us and in using all the individuals we meet in the nativity narratives.

—*David E. Rosage*

II

What Is My Mother's Name?

My mother has many names and many titles.

Formally, I call her "Mother."

Informally, I call her "Mama."

Usually, though, when I'm calling her, I'm crying, "Help!" So then I call her ...

"Our Lady of Prompt Succor"—meaning "Hurry up and help me. I'm in a real tight jam!" Or ...

"Our Lady of Perpetual Help"—meaning that I know she will always help me, no matter how silly my problems are compared to the problems of the rest of the world. Or ...

"Our Lady of Peace"—meaning that if I would only listen, quietly, I could hear so much. Or ...

"Our Lady of the Rosary"—meaning that she has given me a help to solve my problems. Or ...

"Our Lady of the Atocha"—meaning that she wants to remind me that I only ask her for things because she is the Mother of the "Child Who Moves Hearts." ... She reminds me that, although I honor her, I am always to direct my love to her divine Son....

This is what I call my Mother.

This is a Litany of Mary.

—Ann Ball

12

Unstained Explained

The specific type of love we accord to God and God alone is called *latria*. This is the adoration and love of the one divine Entity. To the saints, we accord a love called *dulia*. We honor, love, respect them, and ask their aid (intercession) because they have been set aside by God through their relationship with Him. For Mary, *hyperdulia* is the type of love we have. Just as with all the saints, we honor her, love and respect her, and ask her intercession. Her love is "hyper," or above, that of the other saints because we believe that God, through His will, gave her a status not enjoyed by anyone else.

Catholics believe that Mary was conceived without the stain of original sin, which was the lot of all of the rest of mankind from the time of the fall from grace of the first man. Nonetheless, this woman conceived without sin was asked by God if she would consent to be the Mother of His Son. Mary could have said no! Just like all of mankind, Mary was given free will. At the Annunciation, Mary gave her consent in her *fiat:* "Let it be done to me according to your word."

—*Ann Ball*

13

Gabriel's Greeting

There is sent from God unto the Virgin Mary the Angel Gabriel, whose name means "Strong-man-of-God." For he came as the messenger of Him, who was pleased to appear weak in order that He might prevail against the prince of the power of the air…. It was assigned to the Strong-man-of-God to announce that the Lord of hosts, mighty in battle, was coming to wage war against the powers of the air.

"And the Angel came in unto her, and said: Hail, thou that art full of grace; the Lord is with thee…."

Appropriately is she styled "full of grace" who has attained a grace gained by no other—that of conceiving and bringing forth the actual Author of grace.

—*The Venerable Bede*

14

Rejoice! Herald Tidings of Good

In what words did the angel break the happy news of Redemption? "Hail, thou that art full of grace, the Lord is with thee." [In the original this word *hail* is *chairé*, which means "rejoice."] The messenger of joy in his first word bids her to rejoice. He knew well that his message was of good tidings of great joy to … all creatures…. He knew well that it blunted the sting of death. He knew well that it broke the power of corruption. He knew well that it brought victory over hell…. Therefore, when he began to speak, he spoke in tones of rejoicing, and opened his message with sounds of gladness. Therefore he made the name of joy to herald the tidings of good, which were to be for a joy unto all people, whosoever should believe.

—*Saint Sophronius*

15

Mary's Initial Response

Mary responds initially with fear. "She was deeply troubled by the angel's words, and wondered what his meaning meant." Gabriel responds, "Do not fear, Mary. You have found favor with God." The Scriptures say two things about fear: "The fear of the Lord is the beginning of knowledge" and "Perfect love casts out all fear." Fear can be both compelling and crippling. Somewhere between these two extremes is wisdom. In all the infancy narratives, the servants of God respond with an awe-filled fear. In all the accounts, the angel of the Lord says, "Be not afraid." Jesus himself encourages his disciples to "Be not afraid" many times. We should know the fear of God which brings us to God's love, but once we know this love, all crippling fear is gone. We believe all things in this love.

Mary also questions: "How can this be since I do not know man?" Zechariah questions and it is counted to him as doubt. Mary questions and it is counted as faith. The psalmist says, "I pondered and my spirit questioned." It is all right to question God and to ponder as long as it is done with faith rather than doubt.... Mary questioned, but she never lost faith.

—*John Michael Talbot*

16

The Mystery of the Incarnation

[Gabriel] said then, "The Holy Spirit will come upon you, and the power of the Most High will overshadow you." What does [this] mean? ... Who indeed can [grasp this] except perhaps she who alone deserved to have this most blessed experience?...

"The Holy Spirit will come upon you" means "you will become pregnant by his power." And the words, "The power of the Most High shall overshadow you," mean "the means by which you are to conceive by the Holy Spirit is that the power of God and the wisdom of God, Christ, will be so concealed and so hidden in the shadowing of this most secret counsel that it shall be known only to him and to you." It is as if the angel replied to the Virgin, "Why ask me about something which you are going soon to experience in yourself? You will find out, you will find out, how happily you will find out, and your teacher will be none other than he who works this [within you]. I have been sent only to announce this virginal conception, not to bring it about. This is something which can only be taught by the giver, and learnt only by the receiver."

—*Saint Bernard of Clairvaux*

17

God Asks to Be Born of Woman

[Mary] was not a helpless instrument in salvation history. She was free to say no. When in Greek mythology the god Zeus set out to seduce Europa, he embarked on a course of deception in order to win her affection and abduct her.... The Annunciation was not an act of seduction but a free invitation to a woman to participate in God's salvific action....

The God of the Annunciation is a God who submits himself to the human will, made manifest in the will of one who has no power and no authority in this world. He is a God who asks to be born of a woman. God sought the permission of a representative of the human race before he came to dwell among us—to do otherwise would have been to override human freedom—but the one appointed to speak on behalf of all people and of all history, the one who represents human freedom before God, was a young Jewish girl, who in her femaleness, her youth and her Jewishness, was as far removed from the powers of this world as it is possible to be.

—*Tina Beattie*

18

One Son, Two Natures

"Therefore the Holy to be born of you will be called the Son of God." This means: He who comes from the bosom of the Father into your womb will not only overshadow you, he will even take to himself something of your substance. He who is already the Son of God begotten of the Father before all ages will henceforth be acknowledged to be your son as well. In this way, the son born of God will be yours, and the child born of you will be God's, in such a way that there be not two sons, however, but only one. And although he has one [nature] of you and another of God, yet you will not each have your own son, but he will be the one Son of you both.

"And therefore the Holy to be born of you will be called the Son of God." Please notice how reverently he says "The Holy to be born of you." Why does he say simply the "Holy" and nothing else? I think that it must have been because there was no name by which he could correctly or worthily qualify that extraordinary, that magnificent, that awesome being who was going to unite the Virgin's most chaste flesh to his own soul in the only begotten Son of the Father.

—*Saint Bernard of Clairvaux*

19

Our Lady Full of Grace

Our Lord showed [me] Our Lady Saint Mary at the same time
   (which is to signify the exalted wisdom and truth she had
   in contemplating her Creator
      so great,
      so high,
      so mighty,
      and so good).

This greatness and this nobility of her vision of God filled her
with reverent fear
   and with this she saw herself
      so little and so lowly,
      so simple and so poor, in relation to her Lord God,
   that this reverent dread filled her with humility.

And thus, for this reason, she was filled full of grace
   and of all kinds of virtues
   and surpasses all creatures.

—*Julian of Norwich*

20

May I Have the Heart of Mary

I have come to realize (with John of the Cross and others) that there is an emptiness in my heart that I constantly seek to fill—either with little "needs" or with activity. This passion to fill betrays the fact that I do not want to face and accept my radical emptiness as a creature—as one who is nothing but *capacity* for the infinite. The passion to keep filling more and more is simply a testimony that "You have made our hearts for you, and they are restless until they rest in you."

The psalmist said it long before Augustine: "In God alone is my soul at rest" (Ps 62:1). And Jesus said that in him we would find rest for our souls. Often, when I begin to pray—that is, when I enter that space of God which is supposed to be empty of other things—I find my heart and mind rushing immediately to some "filler"—a need unmet or an activity undone. This simply shows how much my ego fears to be empty. But empty it must be if you, Lord, are to fill it—for that is what you want to do.

May I have the heart of Mary, empty of all and filled with the All which is you.

—*George T. Montague, S.M.*

Not as Men Build Temples

… Not as men build unto the Silent One—
With clang and clamor,
Traffic of rude voices,
Clink of steel on stone, / And din of hammer;—
Not so the temple of thy grace is reared.
But—in the inmost shrine
Must thou begin, / And build with care
A Holy Place, / A place unseen,
Each stone a prayer.
Then, having built, / Thy shrine sweep bare
Of self and sin,
And all that might demean;
And, with endeavor,
Watching ever, praying ever,
Keep it fragrant—sweet, and clean:
So by God's grace, it be fit place—
His Christ shall enter and shall dwell therein
Not as in earthly fane—where chase
Of steel and stone may strive to win
Some outward grace—
Thy temple face is chiseled from within.

—*John Oxenham*

22

The First Eucharist

God so loved the world that he gave his Son. This was the first Eucharist: the gift of his Son, when he gave him to Our Lady, establishing in her the first altar.

Mary was, from that instant on, the only one who was able to affirm with complete sincerity, *This is my body.* She offered her body, her strength, her whole being, to form the body of Christ.

It was on her that the power of the Holy Spirit rested, and in her that the Word became flesh. Mary gave herself to him completely because she had previously consecrated herself to him—in order to preserve … her purity pure, and her chastity chaste, and in order to offer them to the only living God.

When the angel announced to Mary the coming of Christ, she only posed a question: she could not understand how she could take back the gift of herself that she had made to God. The angel explained it, and she understood immediately. Her lips uttered a beautiful response that asserted all that she was as a woman: "I am the servant of the Lord. Let it be done to me as you say."

—*Mother Teresa*

31

23

Ave Maria Gratia Plena

Was this His coming! I had hoped to see
A scene of wondrous glory, as was told
Of some great God who in a rain of gold
Broke open bars and fell on Danae:
Or a dread vision as when Semele
Sickening of love and unappeased desire
Prayed to see God's clear body, and the fire
Caught her brown limbs and slew her utterly:
With such glad dreams I sought this holy place,
And now with wondering eyes and heart I stand
Before this supreme mystery of Love:
Some kneeling girl with passionless pale face,
An angel with a lily in his hand,
And over both the white wings of a Dove.

—Oscar Wilde

24

Friendship Beyond Competition

The Visitation is often portrayed in a way that reinforces a certain dreary image of women as submissive and dutiful caregivers, with the young Mary ignoring her own discomfort to go and help her older cousin. I imagine Mary setting out with wings on her heels to seek the companionship of the one person in all the world who would understand the uniqueness of her situation, and who would share in the delight of her pregnancy. In going to stay with Elizabeth, she found refuge away from the gossiping women of Nazareth in the presence of a woman who was in every sense her soulmate. In Mary and Elizabeth we see the power of a friendship that was not a duty or a burden but a joyful expression of mutually affirming love.

The disciples of Jesus were often locked in competition with one another for first place. There was no such rivalry between Mary and Elizabeth. Elizabeth recognized immediately the primacy of Mary's calling, and her greeting to Mary was a radiant expression of generosity toward the younger woman. John the Baptist would inherit his mother's humility, saying of Jesus, "I am not fit to kneel down and undo the strap of his sandals" (Mk 1:7).

—*Tina Beattie*

Secret Signs, Open Praise

Proclaimed Queen and Mother of a God,
The Light of earth, the Sovereign of saints,
With pilgrim foot up tiring hills she trod,
And heavenly stile with handmaids' toil acquaints;
Her youth to age, her health to sick she lends;
Her heart to God, to neighbor hand she bends....

Eternal lights enclosed in her breast
Shot out such piercing beams of burning love,
That when her voice her cousin's ears possessed
The force thereof did force her babe to move:
With secret signs the children greet each other;
But open praise each leaveth to his mother.

—*Robert Southwell, S.J.*

26

The Song of Mary

My soul doth magnify the Lord,
My spirit rejoiceth greatly
In God my Savior and his word;
For he hath seen the low degree
Of me his handmaiden truly.
Behold now, after this day,
All generations shall speak of me,
And call me blessed always.

For he that is only of might
Hath done great things for me;
And holy is his name by right:
As for his endless mercy,
It endureth perpetually,
In every generation,
On them that fear him unfeignedly,
Without dissimulation.

He showeth strength with his great arm,
Declaring himself to be of power;
He scattereth the proud to their own harm,

Even with the wicked behavior
Of their own hearts every hour
He putteth down the mighty
From their high seat and great honor,
Exalting them of low degree.

The hungry filleth he with good,
And letteth the rich go empty,
Where his own people want no food:
He thinketh upon his mercy,
And helpeth his servant truly,
Even Israel, as he promised
Unto our fathers perpetually,
Abraham and to his seed.

—*Miles Coverdale (Lk 1:46-55)*

27

Mary Claims No Special Place

"My soul doth magnify the Lord, and my spirit hath rejoiced in God my Saviour." Observe, she does not speak of God by any of these titles which would express His newly-created and more intimate relations with herself, but only by those which belonged to her in common with the rest of mankind. God was now her Son; she bore Him in her womb. She had been made, too, in an especial sense, the Spouse of God. Yet she is still the same humble "Handmaid of *the Lord,*" as she was before, and she rejoices in God "Her *Saviour,*" thereby proclaiming that truth which the Church has never ceased to teach, that whatever gifts and privileges might have been bestowed upon her, they were all entirely due to the merits of the Passion and Death of her own Son. For in herself she is nothing, and has nothing; and it was her deep consciousness and hearty acknowledgment of this truth which won her the special regard of God: "He hath regarded the humility of His handmaid."

—*J. Spencer Northcote*

28

Mary Sings of Blessing

"Behold, from henceforth all generations shall call me blessed." … No matter what might happen in any future age of the world to the end of time, nothing could ever blot out the memory of this "great thing" which had now been done to her—nothing could ever eclipse the brightness of this high and incommunicable privilege.… "All generations shall call me blessed." And all the church, until at length it has come to be a part of her very name, which is seldom or never used without this prefix, "the Blessed Virgin." What St. Ildephonsus said many centuries ago may be repeated with still greater emphasis today—"Look throughout the whole world, wheresoever the sun shines, and see if there be any nation or people among whom are no believers in Christ, and wheresoever Christ is confessed and worshipped, and there the venerable Mary, Mother of God, is proclaimed as blessed. By the whole world, and in every tongue, is Mary blessed; all mankind is witness to the truth of this prophecy; she alone foretold it, all mankind is accomplishing it."

—J. Spencer Northcote

29

An Old Song Made New

The prophecy of Mary goes beyond what is merely personal to herself. After having poured forth her gratitude, published her greatness, and foretold her glory, she next draws a rapid but very striking picture of one of the great characteristics of God's work which was now begun…. "He hath showed might in His arm; He hath scattered the proud in the conceit of their hearts. He hath put down the mighty from their seat, and hath exalted the humble. He hath filled the hungry with good things, and the rich He hath sent empty away." It is impossible, in reading this part of Mary's hymn, not to be struck with its close resemblance to the canticle of Anna [Hannah], the mother of Samuel, sung more than a thousand years before. Some few passages in the one seem almost taken from the other; at any rate, the same general sentiment between the songs of Anna and Mary is easy. They are in truth the same canticle, ever new yet ever old; the hymn of grateful thanksgiving, sung to commemorate the triumph of God over His enemies by means of some feeble instrument, whose very weakness only serves to show forth more strikingly His power.

—*J. Spencer Northcote*

30

Revolutionary Carol

Like Hannah, Mary
knew how to sing
the topsyturvey upsidedownside
good news carol
for the poor and hungry,
victimized, oppressed.

At our eternal peril
we choose to ignore
the thunder and the tenor
of her song,
its revolutionary beat.

—*Thomas John Carlisle*

31

The Model of Interior Souls

During the period between the Annunciation and the Nativity, Our Lady seems to me to be the model of interior souls: those whom God has called to live within themselves, in the depths of the bottomless abyss. In what peace and recollection did Mary live and act! The most trivial actions were sanctified by her, for, through them all, she remained the constant adorer of the Gift of God. Yet that did not prevent her from spending herself for others when charity required it. The Gospel tells us that "Mary, rising up ... went into the hill country with haste to a city of Judah," to visit her cousin Elizabeth. Never did the ineffable vision which she contemplated within herself lessen her charity for others, because, says one writer, "though contemplation is directed to the praise and the eternity of its Lord, it possesses and will never lose concord."

—Sister Elizabeth of the Trinity

32

Mother of Our Joy

I salute thee, O full of grace, our Lord is with thee. I salute thee, O cause of our joy, through whom the sentence of our condemnation was revoked and changed into one of blessings. I salute thee, O temple of the glory of God, sacred dwelling of the King of heaven. Thou art the reconciliation of God with men. I salute thee, O Mother of our joy. Truly thou art blessed, for thou alone among all women was found worthy to be the Mother of thy Creator. All nations call thee Blessed.

—*Saint Methodius*

43

33

Let My Future Shine

At morn, at noon, at twilight dim,
Maria, thou hast heard my hymn:
In joy and woe, in good and ill,
Mother of God, be with me still.
When the hours flew brightly by,
And not a cloud obscured the sky,
My soul, lest it should truant be,
Thy grace did guide to thine and thee.
Now, when storms of fate o'ercast
Darkly my present and my past,
Let my future radiant shine
With sweet hopes of thee and thine.

—*Edgar Allan Poe*

34

Immensity Cloistered in Her Womb

Salvation to all that will is nigh;
that All, which always is All every where,
Which cannot sin, and yet all sins must bear,
Which cannot die, yet cannot choose but die,
Lo, faithful Virgin, yields himself to lie
In prison, in thy womb; and though he there
Can take no sin, nor thou give, yet he will wear
Taken from thence, flesh, which death's force may try.
Ere by the spheres time was created, thou
Wast in his mind, who is thy Son, and Brother;
Whom thou conceiv'st, conceived; yea thou art now
Thy Maker's maker, and thy Father's mother;
Thou hast light in dark; and shut'st in little room,
Immensity cloistered in thy dear womb.

—John Donne

35

Yes to New Life

As a way into the Christmas story, the Perfect Pregnancy makes a lousy metaphor. As an exploration of our faith, it makes an even worse one. Mary was young, unwed (though engaged), and she lived in dangerous times. She learned about her pregnancy in a way others found hard to believe. We read that "Joseph was minded to put her away" (Mt 1:19, KJV). She could have been deserted by him, stoned to death for adultery or fornication. There was nowhere safe to have the baby and she ended up delivering in a stable. Soon she would have to move, and at some time she and Joseph had to flee Herod's troops. Sons were (like today) the most likely to die young—under Roman rule no spirited young Jew was safe.

The amazing thing is that in spite of the less-than-ideal circumstances, the sickness, fatigue, miscarriages, stillbirths, and births of children with [physical] problems … as well as the deaths of our children from illness and on the roads, women are prepared to go on risking the heartache of pregnancy and childbirth for the joy of seeing new life come into the world.

That is what Mary said yes to, not the rosy picture of the baby food ads—and this is the real example of a faith in things hoped for, but far from certain.

—*Anna Briggs*

36

Mother of God

Mary is called *Theotokos,* or "God-bearer." This term was first officially used by the church in 431 A.D. at the Council of Ephesus. This particular council was concerned, not so much with Mary, but with the deity of Jesus Christ. Mary is called the Mother of God, not to imply that she is equal to or greater than God, but to emphasize that Jesus, her Son, is God the Son. This does not imply that Mary pre-existed God, or that she cosmically gave birth to God. This would destroy God's timeless and eternal nature, and elevate Mary to actually take the place of God. Mary gives birth on earth to the Son who is eternally begotten of the Father in heaven. Mary is the vessel of the incarnation on earth of what happens eternally within the Trinity in heaven. Mary is only important because Jesus is more important.

As Paul says, "God sent his Son born of a woman, born under the law, to deliver from the law those who were subjected to it, so that we might receive our status as adopted sons." Mary gives birth to the Eternally Begotten, so that all the world might be begotten of God....

Does our understanding and devotion to Mary lead us to these awesome mysteries of God?

—*John Michael Talbot*

37

Song of the Ship

There comes a ship a-sailing
With angels flying fast;
She bears a splendid cargo
And has a mighty mast.
This ship is fully laden,
Right to her highest board;
She bears the son from heaven,
God's high eternal Word.
Upon the sea unruffled
The ship moves in to shore,
To bring us all the riches
She has within her store.
And that ship's name is Mary
Of flowers the rose is she,
And brings to us her baby
From sin to set us free.
The ship made in this fashion,
In which such store was cast,
Her sail is love's sweet passion,
The Holy Ghost her mast.

—*Tauler*

38

Praying toward an Event

When we become fully mindful, as Mary is, both of the power of God and of our own powerlessness, we approach the holy season of Christmas and we understand how much there is in the world that we would change if we could, but which we are powerless to change. We need, fully, to surrender to the Lord's working in our lives, and at the same time, we need fully to hope for the coming of the kingdom here and now.

This kind of prayer, tied to a season, which carries us through and into an event—praying through Advent, toward Christmas, or through Lent, toward Easter and beyond—reminds us of how particular our lives are, how we are creatures of time. By imagination we can become even more connected to reality if we ride with Mary on her journey from Galilee to Bethlehem, waiting to bring the Christ child to birth. When we make such a spiritual journey with vivid imagination, we come across our own impatience. We are faced with a longing to get on with it, to conclude, to arrive somewhere, to know that our time has been well spent, that the time we are spending is not spent in vain....

Hope is the child that Mary bears. Hope is the child we too can bear, in our thoughts, in our actions, in our lives.

—*Emilie Griffin*

39

Another Street, Another Door

St. Joseph:
> "Another street we'll try,
> A courtyard there may be
> Here, before mine eye
> Is this grand hostelrie."

Mary, the Virgin:
> "Prithee, of your grace,
> No further can I go.
> Alone seek you a place;
> My strength it faileth so."

St. Joseph:
> "Hostess dear and kind,
> Pray, of your great pitie,
> Some little corner find,
> To lodge my faint ladie!"

The Hostess:
> "Common folks and poor
> In here we never keep.
> Try that other door;
> 'Tis there such people sleep."

—*Ancient Carol*

40

Mother of Christ

Mother of Christ, Mother of Christ,
The world will bid Him flee,
Too busy to heed His gentle voice,
Too blind His charms to see.

Then, Mother of Christ, Mother of Christ,
Come with thy Babe to me;
Tho' the world be cold, my heart shall hold
A shelter for Him and for thee.

—A Notre Dame Hymn

The May Magnificat

May is Mary's month, and I
Muse at that and wonder why....

Ask of her, the mighty mother:
Her reply puts this other
  Question: What is Spring?—
  Growth in every thing— ....

Well but there was more than this:
Spring's universal bliss
  Much, had much to say
  To offering Mary May.

When drop-of-blood-and-foam-dapple
Bloom lights the orchard-apple
  And thicket and thorp are merry
  With silver-surfed cherry....

This ecstasy all through mothering earth
Tells Mary her mirth till Christ's birth
  To remember and exultation
  In God who was her salvation.

—*Gerard Manley Hopkins*

42

Deliverance

And so it was, that, while they were there, the days were accomplished that she should be delivered (Lk 2:6, KJV).

> It is time.
> My body's clock gongs
> your salvation's hour.
> The water has left the pasture and
> flowed toward the river's mouth.
> Follow or you will wither
> in the desert that remains.
> I will bleed for you
> on this your first dark journey
> but, in time, when life pushes you
> headlong through black canyons
> the wounds will be your own.
> May you learn early:
> At the end light always shines.
> It is here, child;
> the time is come.
> Breathe.

—*Evelyn Bence*

43

Endeavor to Imitate

Put yourself into the company of shepherds, and ... dispose yourself for the invitation of angels, to go and behold ... your Saviour and Redeemer.

1. Consider the Blessed Virgin ... being come to Bethlehem....

2. Jesus … was born in a stable, all other houses refusing his Blessed Mother and him, because they were poor.

3. Behold the wonderful poverty this Blessed Company was reduced unto: he who provides for all creatures in all abundance, feels the misery and want of all things.

4. See the Blessed Mother seeking ... to defend her happy infant from the injuries of a most sharp season ... wrapping the ... maker of all things, in a few simple cloths ....

5. Holy Joseph ... reflected upon the vision made to the Patriarch Joseph, who, in his dream seemed to behold the sun, moon, and stars adoring him. This vision our holy Saint Joseph with great humility applied to sweet Jesus ... who was infinitely respected by his heavenly Father ... and adored by the Blessed Virgin his Mother, and by choirs of angels.

6. Endeavor to imitate ... our Blessed Saviour and his holy Mother, by exercising (at least sometimes) acts of poverty, to wit the want of some commodity; and also of humility, by preferring others before yourself. And certainly know, that unless you practice yourself in these virtues, you shall not obtain them, much less the reward due unto them.

—*Sabine Chambers*

44

God Might Have Skirted the Natural

Behold ... how on that Christmas night God honored childhood. Christ might have made His first visit to our world in a cloud, as He will descend on His next visit in a cloud. In what a chariot of illumined vapor He might have rolled down the sky, escorted by mounted cavalry, with lightning of drawn sword. Elijah had a carriage of fire to take him up, why not Jesus a carriage of fire to bring Him down? ... Or Christ might have had His mortality built up on earth out of the dust of a garden, as was Adam, in full manhood at the start, without the introductory feebleness of infancy. No, no! Childhood was to be honored by that advent. He must have a child's light limbs, and a child's dimpled hand ... and babyhood was to be honored for all time to come, and a cradle was to mean more than a grave....

Behold also that on that Christmas night God honored motherhood. Two angels on their wings might have brought an infant Saviour to Bethlehem without Mary's being there at all.... In some unexplained way, the child might have been found in some comfortable cradle of the village. But no, no! Motherhood for all time was to be consecrated, and one of the tenderest relations was to be the maternal relation.

—DeWitt Talmage

45

The Christmas Symbol

Only a manger, cold and bare,
Only a maiden mild,
Only some shepherds kneeling there,
Watching a little Child;
And yet that maiden's arms enfold
The King of heaven above;
And in the Christ child we behold
The Lord of Life and Love.

Only an altar high and fair,
Only a white-robed priest,
Only Christ's children kneeling there
Keeping the Christmas feast;
And yet beneath the outward sign
The inward Grace is given—
His presence, who is Lord Divine
And King of earth and heaven.

—Author Unknown

46

Jesus Presented at the Temple

Hail to the Lord who comes, comes to his temple gate;
Not with his angel host, not in his kingly state;
No shouts proclaim him nigh, no crowds his coming wait.

But borne upon the throne of Mary's gentle breast,
Watched by her duteous love, in her fond arms at rest,
Thus to his Father's house he comes, the heavenly guest.

There Joseph at her side in reverent wonder stands;
And, filled with holy joy, old Simeon in his hands
Takes up the promised child, the glory of all lands.

O Light of all the earth, thy children wait for thee!
Come to thy temples here, that we, from sin set free,
Before thy Father's face may all presented be!

—*John Ellerton*

47

Forewarned

The first note of warning [of Mary's sorrow] came from holy Simeon: "A sword shall pierce thy soul." These words fell heavily on Mary's heart, that was full of joy and sunshine because of the Babe in her arms. Like a funeral knell this broke in on her joy....: For the old man said: "This child is set for the fall and for the resurrection of many in Israel and for a sign which shall be contradicted, and thy own soul a sword shall pierce, that out of many hearts thoughts may be revealed." Here she is told plainly, though in brief, what Jesus' life is to be. He is set for the fall of many and a sign to be contradicted; and on this account Mary's soul shall be torn with anguish, at seeing her Child battling with the raging storm and finally overwhelmed by it....

[Simeon's prophecy] we call Mary's first sorrow. In reality it includes all her life of sorrow, for it is the lifting of the veil that hung over the future.... This was a revealing to Mary's heroic soul of the sacrifices God would ask of her. God often invites people thus to take up a life of self-denial and reparation.

—*Albert Power, S.J.*

48

Holly Tells a Holy Story

The holly bears a blossom,
As white as the lily flower,
And Mary bore sweet Jesus Christ
To be our sweet Savior.

The holly bears a berry,
As red as any blood,
And Mary bore sweet Jesus Christ
To do poor sinners good.

The holly bears a prickle,
As sharp as any thorn,
And Mary bore sweet Jesus Christ
On Christmas day in the morn.

The holly bears a bark,
As bitter as any gall,
And Mary bore sweet Jesus Christ
For to redeem us all....

Of all the trees that are in the wood,
The holly bears the crown.

—*Traditional Carol*

49

The World's Desire

The Christ-child lay on Mary's lap,
His hair as like a light.
(O weary, weary were the world,
But here is all aright.)

The Christ-child lay on Mary's breast,
His hair was like a star.
(O stern and cunning are the kings,
But here the true hearts are.)

The Christ-child lay on Mary's heart,
His hair was like a fire.
(O weary, weary is the world,
But here the world's desire.)

The Christ-child stood at Mary's knee,
His hair was like a crown.
And all the flowers looked up at Him,
And all the stars looked down.

—*G. K. Chesterton*

50

Let Heaven Reveal …

[Mary might have pondered:] A child—of my own. The one thing I've always wanted, though I haven't imagined it would come like this—at least since the day Mother told me that men seed women in the dark of the night.

A holy child. The one thing Israel has always wanted, though what rabbi would believe my story? How many other women have pushed sons from their wombs and then claimed secret knowledge: He's God's anointed one, sent for such a time as this—to deliver, to reign, just you wait and see?

And the generations waited. The boys grew to be elders who obeyed the commandments, said their prayers, raised their families, and died of old age. Or they became rebels who dreamed of revolution, schemed in dark rooms, rallied in market streets, and died as martyrs for a cause.

Their mothers would have done better to let truth justify itself, let Heaven reveal His plans for their children through some mouth other than their own.

I write this as if it's my own wisdom, when actually most of it is Mother's advice. She tells me—and Joseph—still never to speak of the messengers or messages.

—*Evelyn Bence*

51

Mary as Ark of the Covenant

In [Egypt] there stood ... endless tombstones of dead peoples, granite monuments of their activity....

In this dusty land there came travelling one winter's day a young mother with a new-born child at her breast.... Lo! God Himself is come... into a famine-stricken land to bring plenty to the starving.

And His closest, dearest friend is the woman who holds Him clasped to her breast. Mary is the Ark of the Covenant since she is bearing Jesus, who comes as a Divine Plenipotentiary to effect a new agreement or treaty between God and mankind. This treaty will be ratified by the shedding of the blood of victims....

The Ark in the Old Testament contained objects that were evidence of God's Covenant with His people. Mary—the new Ark—carries the evidence of the new Treaty of Peace concluded between God and man, that evidence being Jesus Himself. Mary had the task of presenting Him to the world....

To soften the shock [of the sin-laden world], His Father gave Him one source of comfort, one deep well of consolation, one human soul to which He could turn from the black, appalling vision of sin and find rest for His Heart—that was the Holy Virgin.... And so the Babe, in the midst of this pagan land of Egypt, nestles close to this pure and spotless Maiden.

—*Albert Powers, S.J.*

52

Primal Affections

The child [Jesus] clasped his tiny arms about his mother's neck, or laid his little hand into the strong hand of Joseph, as they walked on the long road to Egypt, with the same simple desire to utter love and to find love which is the first sign of Life akin to their own that millions of parents' hearts have leaped to recognize in their first-born. [We don't understand] the dignity and unity of all God's vast creation [if we are] offended or distressed when … told that in the Lord of Life these primal affections were of the same sort with those which make the beauty of the life of the beings which are less than [human]. Even the dog, the bird, the lion, know these first instincts of companionship which found their consummate exhibition upon earth when the Son of Mary clung to a human mother with a human love.

—*Phillips Brooks*

53

Mary as Refugee in Egypt

[Mary ponders:] I thought a lot today about this exile and the burden I lay at the feet of our stargazing visitors. If only they [the Wise Men] hadn't stopped in Jerusalem. If only they hadn't made such a fuss. Why did Herod have to get wind of the birth of a peasant king? (Oh how clearly I see the wisdom of Mother's original advice to keep my knowings to myself.)

They were surely holy men, who listened for the Lord's voice. And if He told them not to return home by way of Jerusalem, why didn't He tell them to come straight to our house in Bethlehem and stay away from Herod in the first place?

Did the Lord speak and they not hear? Did the Lord mean for them to follow the star nonstop—straight through the capital? Could the Lord of the universe have meant for us to be driven from our home? Could He want such a boy to sing his first songs in a foreign land?

—*Evelyn Bence*

54

Exiles on This Earth

Let thine intercession be with us, O Mother most pure, and come to us in our need as is thy wont. We are exiles on this earth, with our end ever before our eyes, and even now many of us perish; help us by thy prayers, O merciful Maiden, and be always our advocate lest we are lost through our own ill will. Blessed and most holy one, plead for us before God, who was carried in thy womb, that he may be pitiful to us through thine asking. Amen.

—*Maronite Prayer*

55

Our Model for "Holy Remembering"

Luke presents Mary as a model of … holy remembering. Twice he tells us Mary kept all the events she was experiencing, pondering them in her heart (Lk 2:19, 51). We can assume that this was something she did during her entire life. The Greek word for "pondering" means more than remembering. It means comparing what she was experiencing with other events in the past, particularly the events in the sacred history of her people, for God seemed to be doing again in her life what he had done with Abraham and Sarah…. She can teach us to find in the Scriptures a mirror of our own walk with the Lord.

Jesus tells us that the Holy Spirit is given to us to bring back to our memory all that he said and did: "… the Holy Spirit whom the Father will send in my name, will instruct you in everything, and remind you of all that I told you" (Jn 14:26).

Yet each of us has a unique history and a personal memory of that history. Just as the history of God's people reveals God himself to those with eyes of faith, so our personal history can be for us a true revelation of God—*if* we can learn to use our memory in the service of our faith….

Reviewing our lives … enables us to experience humble gratitude and to praise God for all our blessings.

—George T. Montague, S.M.

56

Losing Jesus in the Temple

"Afflicted I may be, it seems, and blest!
I will not argue that nor will repine.
But where delays he now? Some great intent
Conceals him. When twelve years he scarce had seen,
I lost him, but so found as well I saw
He could not lose himself, but went about
His Father's business. What he meant I mused—
Since understand; much more his absence now
Thus long to some great purpose he obscures.
But I to wait with patience am inured;
My heart hath been a store house long of things
And sayings laid up, portending strange events."

   Thus Mary, pondering oft, and oft to mind
Recalling what remarkably had passed
Since first her salutation heard, with thoughts
Meekly composed awaited the fulfilling.

—*John Milton*

57

Mother of an Adolescent

"Son, why hast Thou thus dealt with us?" [Upon finding Jesus in the temple,] Mary called God, the Lord of Angels, her son. Which of the angels would have dared to do so?... But Mary, knowing herself to be His Mother, boldly applied the word *Son* to that Majesty whom the angels do serve with awe; neither did God despise to be called what He had made Himself. For a little after, the evangelist said: "And He was subject unto them." Who to whom? God to men. I say that God, unto whom the angels are subject, and who is obeyed by the principalities and powers, was subject to Mary.

Marvel at both these things, and choose whether to marvel most at the sublime condescension of the Son, or at the sublime dignity of Mary. Either is amazing, either marvelous. That God should obey this woman is a lowliness without parallel; that this woman should rule over God, an exaltation without match.... It is of your Marker that the evangelist said: "And He was subject unto them." Blush, O proud ashes! God humbled Himself; and do you exalt yourself?

—*Saint Bernard of Clairvaux*

58

Faith in the Silent Years

Today, as I contemplate Jesus living and working in Nazareth, I may wonder about such things as: When did Mary first tell him the story of his birth and of the crowded inns and empty stables? How did she teach him about God the Father? How did the thought of his future mission take shape? Why did he spend most of the years of his life in obscurity?

Mary and Joseph did not understand that Jesus believed that the work of his Father should take precedence over his family relationships to them in Nazareth. Perhaps Simeon's words "and you yourself a sword will pierce" may have come back to have special meaning after Jesus was found in the temple after three days of searching for the son who was lost.

These scenes have obvious implications for our own lives, and especially in situations to which the eyes of faith alone can discern the appropriate response. Let us respond prayerfully to the people and situations involved and reverently enter into colloquy with those to whom we are moved to speak and ask for help in developing our own spirituality.

—*James W. Skehan, S.J.*

59

A Son Leaves Home, A Mother Holds On

First night in Cana: Yes, he's here—and with a train of robust and rowdy fishermen he's picked up.... But he's hardly robust. He's half starved, a shadow of what he once was. Eight weeks away from my table and look at him. It's worse than locusts and honey, which would keep some flesh on his bones.

And his eyes. He's ten years older than when he left.

[Jesus] says he had to fast, forty days in the wild. [Cousin] John had recommended a group of caves. Not to worry.

I couldn't help it. I wanted answers: Are you … and John … living off the land … one of the wild prophets … like Jeremiah? Such a future you found in the desert … the promised future?

"The future is full of miracles, and my work is kinder than John's. The crowds are going to dance like wedding guests.

"Come on, Mother, it's time to celebrate, which is what I'm here to do."

—Evelyn Bence

60

A Second Birthing

There is no birth narrative in John's Gospel, but at the beginning of Jesus' public ministry John describes an encounter between Mary and her Son that constitutes a birthing process, as Mary pushes Jesus into a role that he appears not to be ready to assume....

The gift had already been graciously offered and received when Mary agreed to become the mother of Jesus, but this gift remained hidden from history, hidden from the public gaze, until Mary indicated that the time had come for the gift to be revealed. Just as once God waited for Mary's "Yes," so now God waited again. It was Mary who must utter the word that would allow God's will to be played out in history, that would allow him to reveal his glory to the world....

"Do whatever he tells you," Mary told the servants, and we hear in her words a distant echo of her words to the angel in Luke: "Let what you have said be done to me." When humanity hears and obeys God's Word, God's presence is revealed. Jesus knew, from the way his mother spoke, that his hour had indeed come. Where once she had birthed him in water and blood, now she birthed him again in water and wine.

—*Tina Beattie*

61

Far More Than We Ask

All that [Mary] asked for was just sufficient wine to satisfy the wedding guests. But our Lord changed into wine the contents of six great stone water-pots, which we are expressly told were "filled up to the brim" and contained two or three measures apiece. Moreover, the wine into which He changed the water was of much superior quality. This was so evident, that the chief steward was quite dumbfounded and could not account for it....

Had [the steward] seen what had taken place, he would have realized that when Jesus complied with His mother's request, He not only provided a fresh supply of wine, but wine of a far better quality.

So we shall always find it throughout life. Mary, our tender and loving Mother, is not only always ready to come to our aid, in all our difficulties and dangers, but when she takes our case in hand she obtains for us far more than we ask, and in a measure altogether surpassing our highest expectations.

—*Bishop John S. Vaughan*

62

Mary Short-Changed?

The Gospels tell us little about Mary during the public life of Jesus. Some might interpret this as indicating her role was unimportant. But it is worth noting that the evangelists often intentionally create gaps, trusting the reader to fill them in. For example, the parable of the prodigal son ends without Luke telling us whether the elder son decided to enter the banquet or not. Why this omission? Because Luke wants the reader to identify with the elder son: the reader must decide to join the party or not. Similarly, one could argue that there was no need to portray constantly Mary's reaction to the events of Jesus' life. What mother, and certainly what perfect mother, could be indifferent to what was going on? Luke and John give us enough clues to her response that we can reconstruct what it was to see Jesus' public life through Mary's eyes. When Spirit-guided Christians of subsequent ages did just that, they were merely filling in the gap left by the evangelists. Looking at each step in Jesus' journey through Mary's eyes gives us an understanding of her own faith journey. As the model disciple of her Son, she also helps us respond with a deeper faith of the heart.

—*George T. Montague, S.M.*

63

A Noble, Quiet Mission

In all this history we see the picture of a woman belonging to that rare and beautiful class who approach the nearest to our ideal of angelic excellence. We see a woman in whom the genius and fire of the poet and prophetess is tempered by a calm and equable balance of the intellect; a woman not only to feel deeply, but to examine calmly and come to just results, and to act with energy befitting every occasion. Hers are the powers which might, in the providence of God, have had a public mission, but they are all concentrated in the nobler, yet secret mission of the mother. She lived and acted in her son, not in herself. Mary never seems to have sought to present herself as a public teacher; and in the one instance when she sought her son in public, it was from the tremulous anxiety of a mother's affection rather than the self-assertion of a mother's pride. Mary is presented to us as the mother, and the mother alone, seeking no other sphere.

—*Harriet Beecher Stowe*

64

A Life-Long Yes

Mary never took back that initial, radical response: Whatever you want, Lord. That is what gives rich Marian meaning to an episode in Luke that could confuse you, an incident that has misled many a believer down the centuries. Remember the woman who cried to Jesus from the crowd: "Blessed is the womb that bore you, and the breasts you fed on"? Remember Jesus' response? "Blessed rather are those who listen to the word of God and keep it" (Lk 11:27-28). Not the back of his hand to his mother; quite the contrary. Simply, Mary is even more blessed because she ceaselessly said yes to Yahweh than because she gave birth to God's Son. Of course it was a unique, glorious, ecstatic act, lending her flesh forever to the Son of the Most High. But Mary's most admirable gift to God was not the sheer tabernacle of her body. More blessedly still, she laid at God's feet her freely uttered yes—from Nazareth, through Bethlehem, to Jerusalem and beyond. Whatever you want, Lord. She never took it back.

—Walter Burghardt, S.J.

65

Jesus Praised Her Walk

This it was that the Lord praised in [Mary], namely, that she did the will of His Father, not that her flesh had given birth to His Flesh. Be kind enough to give me your attention, my dear brethren. When the Lord amazed the crowd by working signs and wonders, and showing thereby what was veiled in His Flesh, a woman, in the astonishment of her mind, cried out: "Blessed is the womb that bare Thee, and the paps which Thou has sucked." But He said: "Yea, rather blessed are they that hear the Word of God and keep it." That is to say, "Even My Mother, whom you call blessed, has her blessedness from this, that she keeps the word of God; not because it was in her that the Word of God was made Flesh, and dwelt among us, but because she hears and keeps that Word of God by which she was made (John 1:3) and which in her was made Flesh."

—Saint Augustine of Hippo

66

Family Mediator

Jesus' relatives "set out to take charge of him, convinced he was out of his mind" (Mark 3:21). The passage quoted above suggests that Mary was among those relatives, although it is hard to believe that after all she had experienced of Jesus she would have shared their doubts about his sanity. Mary had herself experienced the absurdity and folly of obeying God. She knew that to respond to God meant behaving in ways that the world might find bizarre or anti-social. I think we need to reinterpret Mary's presence among Jesus' fretful relatives....

I find it helpful to imagine Mary visiting the extended family, persuading them to accept her Son's unusual ways, trying to share with them the vision that inspired him and that continued to inspire her. How many of us as mothers have found ourselves in such a role, mediating between family traditionalists and our offspring who opt for radically different lifestyles and values? Mary visited the family as a mediator, trying to explain the rumours that were filtering through about Jesus' behaviour. Mark tells us that he had already scandalized the community, eating with tax collectors and sinners and being accused of blasphemy. Mary evangelized the family. She told them the good news about her Son, and urged them to come and see for themselves.

—*Tina Beattie*

67

Her Feet Shod with Holiness

And, if our faith had given us nothing more
Than this Example of all Womanhood,
So mild, so merciful, so strong, so good,
So patient, peaceful, loyal, loving, pure—
This were enough to prove it higher and truer
Than all the creeds the world had known before.
Virgin, who lovest the poor and lonely,
If the loud cry of a mother's heart
Can ever ascend to where thou art,
Into thy blessed hands and holy
Receive my prayer of praise and thanksgiving
Let the hands that bore our Savior bear it
Into the awful presence of God;
For thy feet with holiness are shod,
And, if thou bearest it, he will hear it.

—Henry Wadsworth Longfellow

68

Grounded in God's Word

Mary is often portrayed as so serene that we wonder if anything ever bothered her. But this is a projection of a stoic image onto a woman who was a strong and passionate Jewish mother. The mysteries of her life, which we ponder in the rosary, are titled precisely, "the joyful, the sorrowful, the glorious." She walked "by faith and not by sight" (2 Cor 5:7). In her faith journey, the circumstances of her life at times might well have been overwhelming: birthing her Son in a stable; fleeing Herod who wanted to kill her child; losing Jesus in the temple; fearing that the people of Nazareth would throw him over the cliff when he returned home during his ministry; standing at the foot of the cross and watching her only Son die. But if she was the typical Jewess, she knew how to process her feelings through the psalms. She knew how to conquer the circumstances by clinging to the God of victory. She was not a reed easily blown over by the slightest breeze. Like the ideal woman of Proverbs, she was "clothed with strength and dignity" (Prv 31:25) and because of her faith she could laugh at the obstacles life threw her way.

—*George T. Montague, S.M.*

69

Approaching the Cross

From the first she had known that her Son was born to trouble. She had not forgotten the sojourn in Egypt and the cause that had brought it about; she could never forget that her Son's life had been saved only at the price of a deluge of infant blood. She had stored in her heart and had often pondered the words of the old man who had held her Child in the temple:

> "Behold this child is set
> For the ruin and for the resurrection
> Of many in Israel
> And for a sign
> That shall be contradicted
> And thy own soul a sword shall pierce
> That out of many hearts thoughts may be revealed."

This had told her clearly what the prophets, she knew, had long since foreshadowed, that her Son was indeed the Saviour, but that many would be His enemies; nay, in the end would seem to conquer Him in their opposition.

So she had gone through the years, her Mother's heart never forgetting; the shadow of the Cross, the background of doom, never wholly out of sight.

—Alban Goodier, S.J.

A Mother's Intuition: A Son's Gethsemane

"Yes—yes—" As the voice that called to [Mary] had been inarticulate, so now was her answer. "Just a minute, my son. Mother's coming!"

A waft of fragrance came to her out of the night. Of course. The garden. If he were in trouble, where else would he go but to … a garden?

She let the fragrance steal about her like an invisible presence. Yes, he was here. Not to be seen or heard, but only felt, as she had once felt the burden of him beneath her breast. "Here I am," she breathed softly. "Mother's here—little one."

She felt the gnarled trunk of an olive tree. She pressed her face hard against it. Pain. She welcomed it, certain that it was out of some peculiar agony that she had heard her son call. Pain. She had welcomed it once, long ago in a stable.

Now here, again, she seemed to enter into her first hour of travail. As his being had once been merged with hers, so hers became suddenly, inexplicably merged into his, and by that same sacrament of pain that had set his spirit free, there came to her also a knowledge of release and a sense of peace.

Blind that she had been, thinking that a mother had to comprehend, when all that was necessary was to love!

—Dorothy Clarke Wilson

71

The Way of Sorrows

Jesus met his mother as he was being led to his execution. Mary did not faint; she did not scream in rage or despair; she did not try to prevent the soldiers from torturing him more. She looked him in the eyes and knew that this was his hour.... Now his sorrow and her sorrow merged in a deep knowledge of the hour in which God's plan of salvation was being fulfilled. Soon Mary will stand under the cross and Jesus will give her to John, his beloved disciple, with the words: "This is your mother" (Jn 19:27). Mary's sorrow has made her not only the mother of Jesus, but also the mother of all her suffering children. She stood under the cross; she stands there still and looks into the eyes of those who are tempted to respond to their pain with revenge, retaliation, or despair....

I am wounded, wounded by experiences of betrayal and abandonment ... wounded too by my inability to reach out to those around me, whether near or far away, and take away their pain.... My true call is to look the suffering Jesus in the eyes and not be crushed by his pain, but to receive it in my heart and let it bear the fruit of compassion.... It is the way Mary chose, and many Marys continue to choose.

—*Henri Nouwen*

72

Friday Vigil

At the cross her station keeping,
Stood the mournful mother weeping,
Where he hung, the dying Lord:
For her soul of joy bereaved,
Bowed with anguish deeply grieved,
Felt the sharp and piercing sword.

Who, on Christ's dear mother gazing,
Pierced by anguish so amazing,
Born of woman, would not weep?
Who, on Christ's dear mother thinking,
Such a cup of sorrow drinking,
Would not share her sorrows deep?

Jesus, may her deep devotion
Stir in me the same emotion,
Fount of love, Redeemer kind;
That my heart fresh ardor gaining,
And a purer love attaining,
May with thee acceptance find.

—Thirteenth-Century Latin Hymn

73

I, with Mary, at the Cross

Am I a stone, and not a sheep,
    That I can stand, O Christ, beneath Thy Cross,
    To number drop by drop Thy Blood's slow loss,
And yet not weep?

Not so those women loved
    Who with exceeding grief lamented Thee;
    Not so fallen Peter weeping bitterly;
Not so the thief was moved;

Not so the Sun and Moon
    Which hid their faces in a starless sky.
    A horror of great darkness at broad noon—
I, only I.

Yet give not o'er
    But seek Thy sheep, true Shepherd of the flock;
    Greater than Moses, turn and look once more
And smite a rock.

—*Christina Rossetti*

74

Entrusted to Mary

"Seeing his mother there with the disciple whom he loved, Jesus said to his mother, 'Woman, there is your son.' In turn he said to the disciple, 'There is your mother.' From that hour onward, the disciple took her into his own home …" (see Jn 19:25-27).

These … words fully show the reason for the Marian dimension of the life of Christ's disciples. This is true not only of John … but it is also true of every disciple of Christ, of every Christian. The Redeemer entrusts his mother to the disciple, and at the same time he gives her to him as his mother. Mary's motherhood, which becomes man's inheritance, is a gift: a gift which Christ himself makes personally to every individual. The Redeemer entrusts Mary to John because he entrusts John to Mary. At the foot of the cross there begins that special entrusting of humanity to the mother of Christ, which in the history of the church has been practiced and expressed in different ways.…

The Marian dimension of the life of a disciple of Christ is expressed in a special way precisely through this filial entrusting to the mother of Christ, which began with the testament of the Redeemer on Golgotha. Entrusting himself to Mary in a filial manner, the Christian, like the apostle John, "welcomes" the mother of Christ "into his own home" and brings her into everything that makes up his inner life.

—*Pope John Paul II*

75

She Helps Create a Home

The word John [the Gospel writer] uses for "woman" is *gune; gune* refers to a wife in familial relationships, in a household, to the one who helps create a home. So, in saying to his mother, "Woman, here is your son," and to the disciple whom he loved, "Here is your mother," John is talking about the new home that we help build up when we enter the community of disciples and take Mary, who typifies what makes a household of faith, into our home. Earlier, at Cana, when Jesus' hour had not yet come, the "woman" had to have faith. But now, at the cross, when Jesus' hour had come, the one he called "woman" now became mother to those who have faith.

William S. Kurz has written that the readers of John's gospel are to identify with the beloved disciple as similarly beloved disciples.... I'd add to Kurz's insight that, precisely because we are the beloved disciples, what Jesus truly has entrusted to us is his mother, the "woman" who now exists to help us become the community of believers.

—*Michael Crosby, O.F.M. Cap.*

76

Tender to the End

Mary, the Mother of the Lord, stood by the Cross of her Son. My only informant of this fact is the holy Evangelist John. Others have written that when the Lord suffered, the earth quaked, the heavens were veiled in darkness, the sun was hidden, and the thief received, after a good confession, the promise of Paradise. John has taught us what the others have not taught us. Upon the Cross He called her Mother. It is reckoned [by John] a greater thing that in the moment of triumph over agony, He should have discharged the watchful duty of a Son to His Mother, than that He should have made gift of the kingdom of heaven. For if it be a sacred thing to have forgiven the thief, this so great kindness of the Son to the Mother is to be worshipped as the outcome of a tenderer and more touching love.

—*Saint Ambrose*

77

Behold Your Mother

Mary is mother not only of Jesus but of his brothers and sisters as well. This is not pious pap. Good Scripture scholars will tell you that when the crucified Christ murmured "Here is your mother" (Jn 19:27), he was speaking not only to the apostle John but to all who by believing in Jesus are reborn in his image. Here, good friends, is *your* mother whose yes to an angel was a yes for you, a mother who knows what it means to be crucified, a mother who in this vast communion that reaches from earth to heaven is singularly powerful with her Son, a mother who cannot be deaf to our old familiar prayer: "Remember, O most gracious Virgin Mary, that never was it known that anyone who fled to thy protection, implored thy help, or sought thy intercession was left unaided." I am not asking you to worship Mary; that's for pious heretics. I am only asking you to say hello to your mother—a wonderful Jewish mother!

—*Walter Burghardt, S.J.*

78

Welcomed into the Disciples' Home

Mary is the woman of Genesis 3:15 whose offspring will overcome the serpent. She is also the embodiment of Mother Jerusalem, bringing forth the new generation of God's children, represented by the beloved disciple.

We read at the conclusion of the Calvary scene: "And from that hour the disciple took her into his home." The Greek literally means, "The disciple welcomed her into the things that were his own." He *welcomed* her. The evangelist has just proclaimed, in a subtle way, that the new birth of the people of God has taken place. Mary is not only mother of the Savior on the cross. She is now mother of the disciples. And the beloved disciple is a model disciple in welcoming her.

The Gospels are filled with examples of persons who remained obtuse to the gifts Jesus offered, or even rejected them. Even some of his own disciples left him when he offered them the Eucharist (Jn 6:66). But the beloved disciple proves to be keenly aware of the preciousness of this gift: "Jesus has made his own mother my mother!" The disciple takes her into the things *that were his own,* that is, into the treasury of his heart.

We too are invited to welcome Mary as the beloved disciple did.

—*George T. Montague, S.M.*

79

Consider Contemplation

You and I had better begin treating Mary as our mother. Now the way you live such a relationship is not spelled out for you in Scripture; no single way is imposed on you by Rome. Times change and cultures vary; one person's meat is another person's poison. Some go for pilgrimages: to Fatima or Lourdes, to Czestochowa or Guadalupe, to Walsingham or Medjugorje. Others light candles, kneel through novenas, crown Mary Queen of the May. Still others let beads slip insensibly through their fingers, while they praise Mary repeatedly for her yes to God and ask her intercession "now and at the hour of our death." At least we used to.

For me, most meaningful is continual contemplation, with rosary or without. Let reason desist, argument be still, theology fade. Let the mysteries of Mary and her Christ inhabit the screen of your imagination: the face of Mary before a reverent angel or an apologetic innkeeper; her eyes drinking in her newborn baby. Feel how Mary felt when her relatives shouted he was mad, when her neighbors tried to cast him off a cliff....

This is not gushy sentimentalism; this is Christian realism. Here is the flesh-and-blood human who, after her Son on the cross, murmured the most radical yes in recorded history.

—*Walter Burghardt, S.J.*

80

In Appreciation of the Rosary

God has given His children strings of beads,
as we give strings of beads to our children,
to teach them to count.

We do not say,
"Learn from these the doctrine of numbers,
the measure of human life,
the dream of Pythagoras...."

...We say,
"Learn to count on the beads,
small for your hands to hold,
bright for your eyes to see."
And he begins,
slowly,
with one, two, three:
the spark is kindled
to light the flame of philosophy.

God has counted in fifteen Mysteries,
on the fingers of human creatures,
the singleness of the Undivided Love,
the simplicity
that we cannot comprehend....

—*Caryll Houselander*

81

Mary as Martyr

The Martyrdom of the Virgin is set before us, not only in the prophecy of Simeon, but also in the story itself of the Lord's Passion.... "A sword shall pierce through thine own soul also"— Even so, O blessed Mother! The sword did indeed pierce through your soul! For nought could pierce the Body of your Son, nor pierce your soul likewise. Yea, and when this Jesus of yours had given up the ghost, and the bloody spear could torture Him no more, your soul winced as it pierced His dead side—His own soul might leave Him, but yours could not.

The sword of sorrow pierced through your soul, so that we may truly call you more than martyr, in whom the love, that made you suffer along with your Son, wrung your heart more bitterly than any pang of bodily pain could do....

Marvel not that Mary should be called a Martyr in spirit.... [Her Son] could die in the body, and could not she die with Him in her heart? His was the deed of that Love greater than which no man has (Jn 15:13); her deed was of a love like to which no one has, save He.

—*Saint Bernard of Clairvaux*

Mary's Lamentation

"It is my Son I love so much:
For God's sake bury Him nought."
They would not stop though that I swooned,
Till that He in the grave were brought.
Rich clothes they around him wound:
And ever mercy I them besought....

By Him we fell that was my Child.
His sweet mouth well full oft I kissed.
John saw I was in point to spill,
That night mine heart did come to break.
He held his sorrow in his heart still
And mildly then to me did speak:
"Mary, if it be thy will
Go we hence; the Magdalene eke."
He led me to a chamber then
Where my Son was used to be,—
John and the Magdalene also;
For nothing would they from me flee.
I looked about me everywhere:
I could nowhere my Son see.
We sat us down in sorrow and woe
And 'gan to weep all three.

—*Saint Bernard of Clairvaux*

83

After the Burial

Now they being there all alone by themselves, our Lady looking about the house and missing her beloved Son Jesus, with great sorrow of heart … said, "O John, where is now my dear Son that bore so high affection unto you? O Magdalene, Magdalene, where is now your master that so tenderly loved you? O my dear sisters all, where is now my Son? Verily he is gone away from us, he that was all our joy and comfort and the light of our eyes, yea verily, he is gone from us, and that with such exceeding pain and torment as you have all seen: and that which entreateth my sorrow most is, that in all his pains we might not help him, his own disciples forsook him, and his heavenly Father would not succor him, and how soon all these things were contrived against him yourselves are witnesses, for never was there any malefactor so cruelly and speedily put to death as he...."

Then John prayed her to cease of such bitter words and weeping, and comforted her in the best way he could.

And you also by devout imagination.

—*Saint Bonaventure*

84

Easter Dawn

In his manual for directing retreats, *The Spiritual Exercises,* Saint Ignatius Loyola recommends a contemplation of the Risen Jesus that is not explicitly mentioned in the Scriptures: his appearance first of all to his mother, who is not named among the women bringing burial spices to the tomb.

Ignatius' argument for the contemplation of such an appearance follows a long theological tradition that can be traced back to Saint Ignatius of Antioch at the end of the first century: Scripture says Jesus appeared to "many others," and Scripture supposes that we have understanding. Hardly a scientific proof, but Ignatius here and everywhere in the *Exercises* is appealing to the knowledge of the heart. How could Jesus *not* appear first to his mother, since his principal office now is that of consoler as "friends console one another"?

As Mary had been his comforter and consoler from his first breath, so now her Risen Son turns first to her to reveal the greatest of God's wonders: not just a body come back from the dead like Lazarus but a Spirit-filled new creation ushering in a new age for all of us who believe. Like Mary, his mother and ours.

—*John Breslin, S.J.*

85

The Glorious Mysteries

The glorious mysteries point to the victory and glory awaiting all the faithful followers of Jesus....

In contemplating the Resurrection of Jesus, our hearts are filled with joy and gratitude because we are now a redeemed people. Jesus rose from the dead to share his divine life and love with us. Our joyous "alleluias" are heard loud and clear....

Mary's assumption and coronation, the fourth and fifth glorious mysteries, give us even greater reassurance of the possibility of attaining union with God in heaven, where we will reign with Christ forever in our glorified bodies after the universal resurrection from the dead. Mary, a creature like ourselves, was united with her Son in heaven because of her unconditional and persevering commitment to the Lord. Her entrance into heaven, as the model and type of the church, anticipates ours.

Mary's example and dedication show us the way. She is a perfect model of vibrant faith, of persevering prayer, and of total dedication to God. She is our mother pleading before the throne of God for us her children, who are still on our pilgrim journey through life.

—David E. Rosage

101

Mary and the Ascension of Jesus

There was no way for the disciples [and Mary] to avoid the pain of the going of Jesus....

[This] does not mean that we are wrong when we speak of the ascension as one of the "Glorious Mysteries" of Saint Mary. There we are viewing it in its wide bearing.... When the meaning of the ascension became plain, when under the guidance of the Holy Spirit, Saint Mary was able to view her Son as "the One Mediator between God and man, the man Christ Jesus" ... then would all this be to her creative of intense joy. We, seeing so clearly what the ascension essentially meant, can think of it as a mystery of intense joy, but as our Lord passed away from sight the passing would for the moment be one last stab of the sword through this so-often wounded heart.

There would be no lingering upon the hill top. The angel messengers press the lesson that the life before them is a life of eager contest, of energetic action. Jesus had indeed gone in the clouds of heaven, but they were reminded that there would be a reappearance, a coming-again in the clouds of heaven, and in the meantime there was much to do.... Back must they go to Jerusalem and there await the opening of the next act of the drama of the Kingdom of God.

—*J. G. H. Barry*

Joys Seven: A Counting Carol

The first good joy that Mary had,
    It was the joy of one;
    To see the blessed Jesus Christ
    When he was first her son.
The next good joy … It was the joy of two;
    To see her own son, Jesus Christ
    To make the lame to go.
The next good joy … It was the joy of three;
    To see her own son, Jesus Christ
    To make the blind to see.
The next good joy … It was the joy of four;
    To see her own son, Jesus Christ
    To read the Bible o'er.
The next good joy … It was the joy of five;
    To see her own son, Jesus Christ
    To bring the dead alive.
The next good joy … It was the joy of six;
    To see her own son, Jesus Christ
    Upon the crucifix.
The next good joy … It was the joy of seven;
    To see her own son, Jesus Christ
    To wear the crown of heaven.

—*Traditional Carol*

88

There—at Pentecost

The woman who conceived spiritually before she conceived physically, the woman who accepted the Word of God, the woman who was inserted intimately and irrevocably into the mystery of the church, exercises a spiritual motherhood with regard to all peoples....

At Pentecost, the Virgin Mother once again comes forward to exercise her role in union with the apostles, with and in and over the Church. Yet again, she conceived of the Holy Spirit to bring forth Jesus in the fullness of his body, the Church, never to leave him, never to abandon him, but to continue to love and to cherish him through the ages.

This is the woman of history and destiny who inspires us today.

—Pope John Paul II

89

Mary at Pentecost:
The Spirit Comes Again

After the Resurrection and Ascension of Jesus, Mary found her rightful place in the upper room (Acts 1:14) with the others of his inner circle, equally joined with them in the risk and intimacy of prayer, the responsibility for the young church. By faithfulness she had demonstrated her value to God and to his "sent ones." Her suffering had been redemptive.

It took over thirty years—a long testing time for a human. But after the endless, purging pain came the healing love and the rewards of glory: the filling with the breath of God at Pentecost, the tongues of fire, telling both heat and light. That is what happens when any of us says yes to God, as Mary did.

—Luci Shaw

90

Welcome Home, Mother Mary

This day the holy and animated Ark of the living God, which had held within it its own Maker, is borne to rest in that Temple of the Lord, which is not made with hands. David, whence it sprang, leaps before it, and in company with him the angels dance, the archangels sing aloud, the virtues ascribe glory, the princedoms shout for joy, the powers make merry, the lordships rejoice, the thrones keep holiday, the cherubim utter praise, and the seraphim proclaim its glory. This day the Eden of the new Adam receives the living garden of delight, wherein the condemnation was annulled, wherein the Tree of Life was planted, wherein our nakedness was covered....

How was death ever to feed upon her? How was the grave ever to eat her up? How was corruption to break into that body into which Life had been welcomed? For her there was a straight, smooth, and easy way to heaven. For if Christ, who is the Life and the Truth, has said: "Where I am, there shall also My servant be"— how much more shall not rather His mother be with Him?

—*Saint John of Damascus*

91

Mary Lifted from the Dead

Mary lifted from the dead
Living through this glacial blue
Dark with cloud slides overhead
Lift our perished hearts toward you.
     When the winter grew this stern
     And heaven there like Everest,
     What was there we had left to burn
     But the heart within the breast?
What this journey costs the heart
You alone of all best know.
Inch by inch it springs apart
Warped by hot ash white as snow;
     Still the mind can see no path
     Still the soul as cold as ice
     Huddles frozen half to death
     In this ditch near Paradise.
Past the beacon of the sun
Set to light us on our way,
Past the watch-fire of the moon
That holds the beasts of night at bay.
     Mary lifted from the dead ...
     Lifted our perished hearts toward you.

—William Alfred

Robed with the Sun

Who is she that adorned with light,
Makes the sun her robe,
At whose feet the queen of night
Lays her changing globe?
     To that crown direct thine eye,
     Which her head attires;
     There thou mayst her name discrie
     Writ in starry fires.
This is she, in whose pure womb
Heaven's Prince remained;
Therefore, in no earthy tomb
Can she be contained.
     Heaven she was, which held that fire
     Whence the world took light,
     And to heaven doth now aspire,
     Flames with flames to unite.
She that did so clearly shine
When our day begun,
She, how bright her beams decline
Now she sits with the sun.

—*Sir John Beaumont*

93

In Thee Magnificence

Virgin Mother, daughter of thy Son,
    Lowly, and higher than all creatures raised,
    Term by eternal council fixed upon,
Thou art she who didst ennoble man,
    That even He who had created him
    To be Himself His creature disdained not.
Within thy womb rekindled was the love,
    By virtue of whose heat this flower thus
    Is blossoming in the eternal peace.
Here thou art unto us a noon-day torch
    Of charity, and among mortal men
    Below, thou art a living fount of hope.
Lady, thou art so great and so prevailest,
    That who seeks grace without recourse to thee,
    Would have his wish fly upward without wings.
Thy loving-kindness succors not alone
    Him who is seeking it, but many times
    Freely anticipates the very prayer.
In thee is mercy, pity is in thee,
    In thee magnificence, whatever good
    Is in created being joins in thee.

—*Dante*

94

To the Feebleness of Our Prayers...

Is life so rich in sources of help and sympathy and love that we can afford to overpass the eagerness of God's saints to help us, the willingness of the very Mother of God to intercede? Is not the life that shuts out from itself the society of heaven pitifully impoverished?

Too many of us are like the man who owned the field wherein was the buried treasure. Limitless aid is at our disposal, but on condition that we want it and will see it. Let us try to understand what it is to have at our disposal the love and sympathy of the saints of God. They are not remote inhabitants of a distant sphere whose present interests have led to forgetfulness of what they once were, whose present joy is so intense as to make them self-centered. Their very attainment of perfection implies the perfection of their love and the completeness of their sympathy. The perfection of God's saints and their attainment of the end of their course in the enjoyment of the Beatific Vision, has but made them more sensitive of our needs and more eager to help.

The spiritual wisdom and power of the Mother of God is at our disposal today. To the feebleness of our prayers may be added the spiritual wisdom and strength of her intercession.

—J. G. H. Barry

95

Mary as Mediator

[Mary's] unique yes is not simply something to admire, nor did it cease when the angel left her. Her yes did something, and it does something. At the midpoint of history, her yes brought God to birth on earth; it does not cease to link God and man. For the Amen she said to all God willed, this Amen has entered with her into eternity. She still says Amen to the whole ordered plan of redemption; her consent is an eternal yes; and so in some mystery-laden way she continues to share in the redemptive work of her Son.

I admit, it is dreadfully difficult to express what we call the mediation of Mary, how in blood-and-bone reality she can mediate grace without doing violence to the one Mediator. But the fact remains, all of us are in a genuine sense mediators between God and man. God needs men; such is His design for redemption.... All are mediators for all. And in this task of mediation she who gave and gives a unique Amen to Christ has a unique role to play. We do not reach God without her. How, then, can we live without her?

—Walter Burghardt, S.J.

96

Aid Your Child

Mother dear, O pray for me!
While far from heaven and thee
I wander in a fragile bark
O'er life's tempestuous sea,
O Virgin Mother, from your throne,
So bright in bliss above,
Protect your child and cheer my path
With your sweet smile of love.

Mother dear, O pray for me!
Should pleasure's siren lay,
E'er tempt your child to wander far
From virtue's path away.
When thorns beset life's devious way,
And darkling waters flow
Then Mary aid your weeping child,
Yourself a mother show.

Mother dear, remember me,
And never cease your care.
Till in heaven eternally,
Your love and bliss I share.

—*Traditional Hymn*

97

The Hail Mary

Among Catholics, the most common prayer addressed to Mary today is the "Hail Mary." It consists of three parts: the words of the Archangel Gabriel (Lk 1:28) ... the words of Elizabeth under the inspiration of the Holy Spirit (Lk 1:42) ... and a formula of petition, "Holy Mary, Mother of God, pray for us sinners now and at the hour of our death, Amen." The prayer is the result of a gradual development from the sixth century to the sixteenth, when the present wording was adopted. Originally, the prayer consisted only of the twofold scriptural greeting of Mary, but because this seemed incomplete, an element of petition was added. The idea of petitioning Mary, asking her to pray for us ... dates back to at least the third century.

It is important to note that the "Hail Mary" is a scriptural prayer, and that the petition asks Mary to pray to the Lord for us, both now and when we die. Mary is honored as Scripture honors her. She is not worshipped, but simply asked to pray for us.

—*Alan Schreck*

98

A Coptic Prayer

Hail to thee, Mary, the fair dove, which hath borne for us God the Word. We give thee salutation with the Angel Gabriel, saying, Hail, thou that art full of grace; the Lord is with thee.

Hail to thee, O Virgin, the very and true Queen; hail, glory of our race. Thou hast borne for us Emmanuel.

We pray thee, remember us, O thou our faithful advocate with our Lord Jesus Christ, that He may forgive us our sins.

—Prayer from the Coptic Liturgy

99

A Prioress Requests: Guide My Song

O Mother Maid! O Maid and Mother free!
O bush unburnt; burning in Moses' sight!
That down didst ravish from the Deity,
Through humbleness, the spirit that did alight
Upon thy heart, whence, through that glory's might,
Conceived was the Father's sapience,
Help me to tell it in thy reverence.

Lady! thy goodness, thy magnificence,
Thy virtue, and thy great humility,
Surpass all science and all utterance;
For sometimes, Lady, ere men pray to thee
Thou goest before in thy benignity,
The light to us vouchsafing of thy prayer,
To be our guide unto thy Son so dear.

My knowledge is so weak, O blissful Queen!
To tell abroad thy mighty worthiness,
That I the weight of it may not sustain;
But as a child of twelve months old or less,
Even so fare I; and therefore, I thee pray,
Guide thou my song which I of thee shall say.

—*Geoffrey Chaucer, tr. by William Wordsworth*

True Devotion Is…

True devotion to our Lady is *interior;* that is to say, it comes from the spirit and the heart. It flows from the esteem we have of her, the high idea we have formed of her greatness, and the love which we have for her.

It is *tender;* that is to say, full of confidence in her, like a child's confidence in his loving mother. This confidence makes the soul have recourse to her in all its bodily or mental necessities, with much simplicity, trust, and tenderness. It implores the aid of its good Mother, at all times, in all places, and about all things; its doubts, that it may be enlightened; in its wanderings, that it may be brought into the right path; in its temptations, that it may be supported; in its weakness, that it may be strengthened; in its falls, that it may be lifted up….

True devotion to our Lady is *holy;* that is to say, it leads the soul to avoid sin, and to imitate in the Blessed Virgin particularly her profound humility, her lively faith, her blind obedience, her continual prayer….

True devotion to our Blessed Lady is that is to say, it inspires the soul not to seek itself but God only.

—*Louis Marie Grignon de Montfort*

A Spiritual Vision of Mary

Our good Lord looked down on His right side...
    and He said, "Dost thou wish to see her?"...
For after Himself, she is the most blessed sight.
        (But from this I am not taught to yearn to see her bodily presence while I am here, but the virtues of her blessed soul—her truth, her wisdom, her love—whereby I can learn to know myself and reverently fear my God.)...
Often I prayed this and I expected to have seen her in bodily presence, but I saw her not so,
        but Jesus in that word showed me a spiritual sight of her (in the same way as I had seen her before—little and simple—so He showed her now exalted and noble and glorious and pleasing to Him above all created beings).
And so He wishes that it be known that all those that delight in Him should delight in her and in the delight that He has in her and she in Him.

—*Julian of Norwich*

Hear My Prayer

I want some valiant soldier, here,
I want some valiant soldier, here,
I want some valiant soldier, here,
To help me bear the cross.

O, hail, Mary, hail!
O, hail, Mary, hail!
O, hail, Mary, hail!
To help me bear the cross.

Done with the driver's driving,
Done with the massa's hollering,
Done with missus' scolding,
I want some valiant soldier, here,
I want some valiant soldier, here,
I want some valiant soldier, here,
To help me bear the cross.

—*African-American Spiritual*

103

Lead Us Out of Darkness

Mother of God, since we have obtained confidence in you, we shall not be put to shame, but we shall be saved. Strengthened by your help and intercession, O holy, pure, and perfect one, we shall resist our temptations and scatter them. We take up the shelter of your aid as a strong shield. And we pray and beseech you that we may call upon you, O Mother of God, that you preserve us through your prayers. Lead us out of darkness, to glorify the almighty God who took flesh in you. Amen.

—Prayer from the Coptic Office of Sleep

104

Queen of Heaven

Queen of heaven, blessed may thou be
For God's Son born He was of thee,
For to make us free.
Gloria Tibi, Domine.

Jesu, God's Son, born He was
In a crib with hay and grass,
And died for us upon the cross.
Gloria Tibi, Dominie.

To our Lady make we our moan,
That she may pray to her dear Son,
That we may to His bliss come.
Gloria Tibi, Dominie.

—*Sixteenth-Century Prayer*

105

Queen of the Saints

Almost the first public act recorded by St. John in the life of Jesus is this granting of a special, miraculous favour at His Mother's request; just as the last words He addressed to any living mortal were His tender words of farewell to Mary from the Cross, when He asked her to look upon St. John, the disciple whom He loved, as her son.

In the beginning of His public life Mary is thus found asking help for those in need; and at the end of His life she receives a mandate from her Son to undertake the same merciful work for His Church, to plead ever at the throne of Mercy for the wine of peace and joy and consolation for Jesus' friends. In giving her that commission Jesus appointed His Mother Queen of All the Saints.

For if the disciples whom Jesus especially loves are to be her children then she will be solicitous for them with all a mother's tenderness and love, and she will strive incessantly to secure for them a full participation in the supreme blessing which Jesus came to bring from heaven to earth, the blessing of perfect peace and union with God. Of that gift the Angels sang as they surrounded their Queen at Bethlehem on the first Christmas night. "Glory to God in the highest and peace on earth to men of good will."

—*Albert Power, S.J.*

106

Queen of Angels

It is from angel lips that the human race (Mary herself first of all) learned the secret of the Incarnation. An angel first taught the world the lesson of adoring Jesus as God. That was a privilege which God granted to St. Gabriel. And Gabriel teaches us both by words and by example—by his word of reverence to Mary, bidding her have no fear, since she is God's chosen one and is to be the Mother of the Son of God, and by his words describing the marvelous supernatural activity that will bring about this wonder; and then by his attitude of deep reverence and devotion towards Mary, as Mother of the Most High God. "Therefore also the Holy One born of thee shall be called the Son of God."

Hence we turn to the angels to learn Mary's dignity; she is Queen of the Angels, and they will instruct us in the duty of loving and serving her, who is their Queen. They are filled with reverence for their Queen because of her relationship to God Himself. And they see her transcendent beauty as a Child of Grace, beautified by grace beyond all expression.

This, then, is the angels' first duty, to help us to know Jesus as God, to rouse, kindle, and support our faith against the attacks of unbelief.

—Albert Power, S.J.

107

Gateway of Heaven

Mother of God, gateway of heaven to humanity,
with a divine voice the angel declared:
  Hail, full of grace, the Lord is with thee.
He who sitteth with the Father above the cherubim
was pleased to dwell within thy maiden body;
  Hail, full of grace, the Lord is with thee.

He who dwelt amid the flaming seraphim
was seen among men and in a woman's arms;
  Hail, full of grace, the Lord is with thee.

—Prayer from the Armenian Liturgy

108

Our Lady of Mercy

Mary, then, is the one who has the deepest knowledge of the mystery of God's mercy. She knows its price; she knows how great it is. In this sense, we call her the Mother of Mercy, Our Lady of Mercy or Mother of Divine Mercy....

It was precisely this "merciful" love, which is manifested above all in contact with moral and physical evil, that the heart of her who was the Mother of the Crucified and Risen One shared in singularly and exceptionally—that Mary shared in. In her and through her this love continued to be revealed in the history of the church and of humanity.

This revelation is especially fruitful because in the Mother of God it is based upon the unique tact of her maternal heart, on her particular sensitivity, on her particular fitness to reach all those who most easily accept the merciful love of a mother. This is one of the great life-giving mysteries of Christianity, a mystery intimately connected with the mystery of the Incarnation.

—Pope John Paul II

109

A Three-O'Clock Prayer

Fr. Chaminade taught his disciples to renew their consecration [to Mary as their mother] by pausing daily at three o'clock to recall the death of Jesus on Calvary and to enter into the mystery of Jesus' gift of his mother to the church and to each of us....

Although Fr. Chaminade did not write any particular formula for the three o'clock prayer, one was soon fashioned. Today's version goes something like this:

Lord Jesus, we gather in spirit at the foot of the cross with your mother and the disciple whom you loved. We ask your pardon for our sins which are the cause of your death. We thank you for remembering us in that hour of salvation and for giving us Mary as our mother. Holy Virgin, take us under your protection and open us to the action of the Holy Spirit.

St. John, obtain for us the grace of taking Mary into our life, as you did, and of assisting her in her mission. May the Father and the Son and the Holy Spirit be glorified in all places through the Immaculate Virgin Mary. Amen.

—George T. Montague, S.M.

110

Mary Calls Us to Christ

Mary's appearances [such as Guadalupe, Lourdes, and Fatima] share some striking similarities. First, she does not come to the wealthy or learned among us, but rather to the poorest, humblest, most unlearned of her children—to those who would receive her message simply and without question. Second, her message is always the same: Mary calls us to repent of our disobedience to God, to return to a life of prayer and penance, a life of faith and love. Third, to convince us of God's love and mercy, Mary brings his healing to many.

Out of her motherly love and concern for her children, Our Lady comes to warn and to plead. She warns that God's judgment cannot be held off much longer. She pleads with us to accept the salvation offered by her Son Jesus before it is too late. She portrays the anguish and sorrow of a mother who sees her children going down a treacherous path that surely leads to death.

Mary comes particularly for the conversion of sinners. Through Mary's intercession, Christ can move the most hardened of hearts.

—*Pamela Moran*

III

Pleading Prayer for Peace

To Mary, then, who is the Mother of Mercy and omnipotent by grace, let loving and devout appeal go up from every corner of the earth—from noble temples and tiniest chapels, from royal palaces and mansions of the rich as from the poorest hut—from every place wherein a faithful soul finds shelter—from blood-drenched plains and seas. Let it bear to her the anguished cry of mothers and wives, the wailing of innocent little ones, the sighs of every generous heart: that her most tender and benign solicitude may be moved and the peace we ask for be obtained for our agitated world.

—Pope Benedict XV, May 5, 1917
Eight days later, Mary appeared
to three children at Fatima, Portugal.

112

Teach Us to Overcome Fear

Lady of Lourdes, like unto the child to whom thou didst appear, we also are bowed down by fear and terror in the presence of manifestations from on high. When our souls are secretly agitated by something divine, moving us to the fulfillment of some duty, or the practices of religion, we too experience a certain feeling of fear and weakness. Teach us, O Mary, to overcome the first fears of our cowardly nature by the help of prayer. Make us understand that virtue is austere in appearance only, and that if a certain fear goes before the practice of its acts, they are accompanied and followed by ineffable joy....

And when God grants us any special grace, obtain for us that, like the humble shepherdess [at Lourdes], we also may cherish it in our memories and keep it in our hearts, without suffering ourselves to be disturbed by the events, troubles, mockeries, or contradictions of the outer world. [Help us] to make such use of each grace received as thereby to merit a new one; so that advancing from virtue to virtue we may at length arrive at the foot of God's Throne....

Lady of Lourdes, pray for us. Amen.

—*Henri Lasserre*

113

Mary: Health of the Weak

This title [for Mary] may be taken to refer to health of body or of soul; and in both senses Mary deserves the title. Lourdes, with its wonders, proclaims aloud to the whole world her right to be called the Restorer of bodily health; and the conversions innumerable which result from prayer to Our Lady show that she is the Health of the Weak in the spiritual sense. Mary's apostolate has been pre-eminently an apostolate through prayer. Her petitions, ever ascending to God, secure showers of grace for the softening of hard hearts, and the strengthening and comforting of souls already in God's friendship.

The possibility of an Apostleship by means of Prayer rests on the great fact that grace is the force that turns men's souls to God; such an Apostleship rests on the principle that it is not mere natural goodwill or arguments, or mere natural energy, that help to spread Christ's kingdom, but God's own direct influence in the interior realm of the soul. And God works thus interiorly and efficaciously in response to prayer.

—Albert Power, S.J.

Our Lady of Medjugorje

In Medjugorje, the Madonna beseeches that we reach out to God. "Make yourself a new heart and a new spirit! Why should you die?" (Ez 18:31). Presenting her Son for peace and reconciliation, she invites us to celebrate a permanent Christmas. Through conversion, she offers to lead us to the house of peace.

On the third day of the apparitions, when the children asked: "Dear Madonna! Why have you come here?" she answered: "I come to convert and reconcile people." ... Her peace and reconciliation are not just the absence of war; they are guarantors of God's presence. God is the source of her peace, and its true abode is the hearts of men. True peace is fully realized only in God, and must be the object of man's permanent search. Peace cannot be found apart from God. In no sense is it the sole possession of those who are intelligent, rich, and powerful; they must attain it the same way as the foolish, the poor, the powerless....

The Madonna is bringing this peace to Christians, and Christians in turn are called to bring it to all the world. We believe that man will finally find peace when he surrenders to and reconciles himself with God.

—*Svetozan Kraljevic, O.F.M.*

115

The Madonna Prays

Christians have known the Madonna as God's servant since the beginning in Nazareth until this moment, but the children and pilgrims of Medjugorje emphasize "the Madonna who prays." Indeed, the very way of life in Medjugorje is prayer. Everything that is said or done there can be described as a form of prayer, which the Madonna leads and urges everyone to follow....

In answer to a question from a priest about the necessity of forming a prayer group in his parish, she [the Madonna] said: "There is need for a prayer group not only in his but in all parishes. Spiritual renewal is necessary for the entire Church."

... This, then, is the Madonna whom the six children came to know in Medjugorje, the Madonna who prays with us and for us and who calls us to adopt the habit of daily prayer for all our intentions.

Prayer is the way we associate with her and communicate with God. For Christians, certainly, prayer is like being home.

—*Svetozan Kraljevic, O.F.M.*

116

Mary's Many-Sided Mission

Christ is the only way to the Father, and the ultimate example to whom the disciple must conform his own conduct, to the extent of sharing Christ's sentiments, living his life and possessing his Spirit. The church has always taught this and nothing in pastoral activity should obscure this doctrine. But the Church, taught by the Holy Spirit and benefiting from centuries of experience, recognizes that devotion to the Blessed Virgin, subordinated to worship of the divine Savior and in connection with it, also has a great pastoral effectiveness and constitutes a force for renewing Christian living. It is easy to see the reason for this effectiveness. Mary's many-sided mission to the people of God is a supernatural reality which operates and bears fruit within the body of the Church. One finds cause for joy in considering the different aspects of this mission, and seeing how each of these aspects with its individual effectiveness is directed toward the same end, namely, producing in the children the spiritual characteristics of the First-born Son. The Virgin's maternal intercession, her exemplary holiness, and the divine grace which is in her become for the human race a reason for divine hope.

—*Pope Paul VI*

Bearing the Fruit of the Spirit

Mary stands as a symbol of a totally Spirit-controlled sexuality. By her chastity and virginity she says that we are called beyond the mere animal lust of human nature to a more divine passion in Christ. If we say yes to our divine Lover, then, with Mary, we will give birth to the Christ child in our life. We will bear the fruit of the Spirit spoken of by Paul: "Love, joy, peace, patient endurance, kindness, generosity, faith, mildness and chastity.... Those who belong to Christ Jesus have crucified their flesh with its passions and desires. Since we live by the Spirit, let us follow the Spirit's lead!"

This is all fine and good. But how do we free ourselves from such passion and lust?...

Paul treats this subject of vice and virtue concluding, "Dedicate yourselves to thankfulness." ... Mary, herself, manifests the power of the Spirit within her by singing a song of praise. "My soul proclaims the greatness of the Lord." It is through praise and thanksgiving that we stir up the Spirit, and it is through the fire of the Spirit that we overcome the fire of sinful passion and lust.

Do we prefer the impregnation of the Holy Spirit over the sexuality of the world?... When the Spirit conceives, the love of Jesus will daily burn anew in our life.

—John Michael Talbot

118

The Latest Word ...

Whenever I hear about the latest apparition of Mary, which yet again emphasizes people's concern with what she allegedly says or means, I return to John's gospel to listen to the last words he records coming from her lips. For me, these serve as her testament—and God's word to me as well. To be a beloved disciple, I must "do whatever he tells you" (Jn 2:5). And what he tells me, as he entrusts his mother to me as a beloved disciple, is that the future of our church will fulfill his vision when we who have had Mary entrusted to our care begin to entrust ourselves not only to her, but to each other. Then we will have created a home we can call church.

The first hour began when, in the midst of his family and friends, Mary [at Cana] recognized a need and ushered the way for Jesus to perform the first of his signs. Now, as we hear these words of Jesus from the cross [behold your mother/son], the new hour begins when we perform the last of his signs and become the community of disciples that we have been called to be.

—*Michael Crosby, O.F.M. Cap.*

David and Goliath Revisited

Thou art the Sling, thy Son the Stone
That David at Goliath flung;
Eke Aaron's rod, whence blossom sprung
    Though bare it was, and dry:
Tis known to all, who've looked upon
    Thy childbirth wondrous high.

In thee has God become a Child,
The wretched foe in thee is foiled;
That Unicorn that was so wild
    Is thrown by woman chaste;
Him hast thou tamed, and forced to yield,
    With milk from Virgin breast....

Take, Ladye dear, this little Song
That out of sinful heart has come;
Against the fiend now make me strong,
    Guide well my wandering soul.

—*Robert Grossetest*

Mary, Compared to the Air We Breathe

… I say that we are wound
With mercy round and round
As if with air: the same
Is Mary, more by name.
She, wild web, wondrous robe,
Mantles the guilty globe,
Since God has let dispense
Her prayers his providence:
Nay, more than almoner,
The sweet alms' self is her
And men are meant to share
Her life as life does air.
If I have understood,
She holds high motherhood
Towards all our ghostly good
And plays in grace her part
About man's beating heart,
Laying, like air's fine flood,
The deathdance in his blood;
Yet no part but what will
Be Christ our Saviour still.…

—*Gerard Manley Hopkins*

Acknowledgments

1. Emilie Griffin. From "The Solemnity of Mary." Reprinted by permission of the author.

4. From Thomas John Carlisle, *Beginning with Mary*. © 1986 Wm. B. Eerdmans Publishing Co. Reprinted by permission of the publisher.

5. From *The Prayers of Catherine of Siena* edited by Suzanne Noffke, P.O. © 1983. Reprinted by permission of Paulist Press.

6. Pope John Paul II. *Prayers of John Paul II*. © 1996. Reprinted by permission of Servant Publications.

10. From David E. Rosage, *Praying the Scriptural Rosary*. © 1989. Reprinted by permission of Servant Publications.

11. and 12. From Ann Ball, *A Litany of Mary*. © 1988 by Our Sunday Visitor, Inc. Reprinted by permission of the publisher.

15. From John Michael Talbot, *Reflections on the Gospels*. © 1994. Troubadour for the Lord, Rt. 7, Box 608, Eureka Springs, AR 72631. Tel. (501) 253-7710. Reprinted by permission.

16. From Bernard of Clairvaux, Homily IV *Super Missus Est*, translated by Marie-Bernard Said, O.S.B., in *Bernard of Clairvaux: Homilies in Praise of the Blessed Virgin Mary*. Kalamazoo, Michigan: Cistercian Publications, 1993. Reprinted by permission of the publisher.

17. Excerpt from *Rediscovering Mary: Insights from the Gospels* by Tina Beattie, © 1995 by Tina Beattie, published by Triumph Books. Reprinted by permission of Triumph Books (North American rights). U.K. and world rights granted by permission of Burns and Oates.

18. From Bernard of Clairvaux, Homily IV *Super Missus Est*, translated by Marie-Bernard Said, O.S.B., in *Bernard of Clairvaux: Homilies in Praise of the Blessed Virgin Mary*. Kalamazoo, Michigan: Cistercian Publications, 1993. Reprinted by permission of the publisher.

59. Taken from *Mary's Journal,* by Evelyn Bence. © 1992 by Evelyn Bence. Used by permission of Zondervan Publishing House.

60. Excerpt from *Rediscovering Mary: Insights from the Gospels* by Tina Beattie, © 1995 by Tina Beattie, published by Triumph Books. Reprinted by permission of Triumph Books.

62. From George T. Montague, S.M., *The Woman and the Way.* © 1994. Reprinted by permission of Servant Publications.

64. From Walter Burghardt, S.J., *To Christ I Look.* © 1989. Reprinted by permission of Paulist Press.

66. Excerpt from *Rediscovering Mary: Insights from the Gospels* by Tina Beattie, © 1995 by Tina Beattie, published by Triumph Books. Reprinted by permission of Triumph Books (North American rights). U.K. and world rights granted by permission of Burns and Oates.

68. From George T. Montague, S.M., *The Woman and the Way.* © 1994. Reprinted by permission of Servant Publications.

70. Condensed from Dorothy Clarke Wilson, *The Brother.* Rev. ed. © 1984. Published by Thomas Nelson and Sons. Used by permission of the author.

71. From Henri Nouwen, *Walk with Jesus.* © 1990. Reprinted by permission of Orbis Books.

74. From Pope John Paul II, *Mother of the Redeemer.* Reprinted by permission from *Breakfast with the Pope,* © 1995 by Servant Publications.

75. From Michael Crosby, O.F.M. Cap., *The Seven Last Words.* © 1994. Reprinted by permission of Orbis Books.

77. From Walter Burghardt, S.J., *To Christ I Look* © 1989. Reprinted by permission of Paulist Press.

78. From George T. Montague, S.M., *The Woman and the Way.* © 1994. Reprinted by permission of Servant Publications.

79. From Walter Burghardt, S.J., *To Christ I Look.* © 1989. Reprinted by permission of Paulist Press.

80. From Caryll Houselander, *The Flowering Tree*. © 1945. Reprinted with permission of Sheed & Ward, 115 E Armour Blvd., Kansas City, MO 64111. To order, call (800)333-7373.

84. John Breslin, S.J. Used by permission of the author.

85. From David E. Rosage, *Praying the Scriptural Rosary*. © 1989. Reprinted by permission of Servant Publications.

88. Pope John Paul II, *Discourses*.

89. From Luci Shaw, "Yes to Shame and Glory," *Christianity Today*, December 12, 1986. Reprinted by permission of the author.

91. "Mary Lifted from the Dead," by William Alfred. From *American Hymns Old and New*, edited by Albert Christ-Janer, Charles W. Hughes, and Carelton Sprague Smith. © 1980 by Columbia University Press. Reprinted with permission of the publisher.

95. From Walter Burghardt, S.J., *Tell the Next Generation*. © 1980. Reprinted by permission of Paulist Press.

97. From Alan Schreck, *Catholic and Christian*. © 1984. Reprinted by permission of Servant Publications.

101. From *A Lesson of Love: The Revelations of Julian of Norwich*. © 1988 by The Order of Julian of Norwich. Reprinted by permission of Walker and Company, New York, NY. All rights reserved.

108. Pope John Paul II, *Mother of the Redeemer*.

109. From George T. Montague, S.M., *The Woman and the Way*. © 1994. Reprinted by permission of Servant Publications.

110. From Pamela Moran, *Marian Prayer Book*. © 1991. Reprinted by permission of Servant Publications.

114. and 115. Excerpts from *The Apparitions of Our Lady at Medjugorje* by Svetozan Kroljevic, O.F.M., ed. Michael Scanlan, O.F.M. T.O.R. © 1984 by Franciscan Press. Used by permission of the publisher.

116. Pope Paul VI, *Marialis cultus*.

117. From John Michael Talbot, *Reflections on the Gospels.* © 1994. Troubadour for the Lord, Rt. 7, Box 608, Eureka Springs, AR 72631. Tel. (501) 253-7710. Reprinted by permission.

118. From Michael Crosby, O.F.M. Cap., *The Seven Last Words.* © 1994. Reprinted by permission of Orbis Books.

Also of Note

J. G. H. Barry, *Our Lady Saint Mary.* New York: Edwin S. Gorham, 1922.

J. Spencer Northcote, *Mary in the Gospels.* London, Burns and Oates, 1906.

Albert Power, S.J., *Our Lady's Titles.* New York: Frederick Pustet, 1928.

Special thanks for the assistance of Joseph Tylenda, S.J., at the Woodstock Theological Library on the campus of Georgetown University.